A River's Course

A GOURMET COLLECTION
of
The Junior Charity League of Shelby, Inc.
Shelby, North Carolina

A River's Course

The Junior Charity League of Shelby, Inc.
P. O. Box 1325
Shelby, North Carolina 28150

ISBN 0-9759054-0-6

Printed By:

WIMMER
COOKBOOKS

A CONSOLIDATED GRAPHICS COMPANY

800.548.2537   wimmerco.com

Introduction

Dining by water has always held a special lure...

Imagine, if you will, elegant dinners on lakeside decks...
Candlelight and fireflies flickering in the fading summer light...
Springs bubbling a symphony in the background...
Couples, friends, and families dining on savory fare.

Or, perhaps, a blanket spread by a coursing stream...
A well-filled basket of unique and delectable items
Waiting for a family to devour while lounging by
This watery glen.

Whether you are seeking luncheon fare
For your ladies' club...
Sweet treats for little,
And not so little, ones...
Or a special entrée to astound
Your supper club or church fellowship.
In the pages to follow you will find delights
Sure to create those special dining experiences.

Come...be delighted by

A River's Course

Contents

Our Mission

The Junior Charity League of Shelby, Inc. appreciates your
support of our first venture into culinary publishing. The efforts of
over one hundred dedicated women working tirelessly for over a
year resulted in the work that you now hold in your hands. Your
generosity will enable hundreds of less fortunate children
to be supported and clothed.

Our mission is clear…"for I was hungry and you gave me food,
I was thirsty and you gave me drink, I was a stranger and you
welcomed me, I was naked and you gave me clothing." The Junior
Charity League of Shelby, Inc. has been clothing children since
1966. Hundreds of children have been positively impacted by this
quest. Our mission could not be a reality without the
unending support of our community and from those
who contribute to our endeavors.

Know well that with the purchase of this cookbook, you have
helped a child in need. The women of the Junior Charity League
of Shelby, Inc. thank you on behalf of all these deserving children.

Acknowledgements

About the Artist

A self-taught artist, Mary Sparrow Smith was born in North Carolina. As a young child much of her time was spent drawing and painting people and animals. A graduate of St. Mary's College in Raleigh, North Carolina and the University of North Carolina at Chapel Hill, she began her career in art as a graphic artist and illustrator for Spectator Magazine. She ventured out on her own specializing in decorative painting, trompe l'oiel, murals and later, portraits. With the encouragement of her husband, Mary finally pursued a career as a professional portrait artist. Her media include oil, pastel and black and white. Over the years, her recognition has grown. Her portraits hang in private collections throughout the United States. In 2001, Mary extended her advertising through her website. She resides in Shelby, North Carolina with her husband, two sons and daughter.

www.marysparrowsmith.com

About the Cover Art
By Mary Sparrow Smith

Along the northern edge of the Broad River in the southernmost part of Cleveland County, just where the line defines North and South Carolina, the Broad River Greenway celebrates all that the Broad River is to this area. Where prehistoric Native Americans once found sustenance, many now traverse nature's flowing path that leads from the foothills of the Blue Ridge Mountains to the tidewaters of the Atlantic. Come. Ride horses or hike the trails, then stop to grill burgers or flame a marshmallow for s'mores. Enjoy the best of living in the South-hot summers cooled in the water, mild springtime Easter egg hunts by the historic cabin, the get-away-from-it-all feeling of crisp autumn afternoons. Come enjoy the Broad River and its Greenway.

Cookbook Committee 2003 - 2004

Cookbook Chairs
Zuzana Rybnicek
Jean Konitzer

Recipe Chairs
Susan DuBose
Lisa Stachowicz

Testing Chairs
Mary Kelly
Altman Anderson

Design Chair
Becky Teddy

Copy Chair
Kim Lee

Marketing Chairs
Loann Meekins
Cindy Teddy

Business Operations Chair
Sheila Allen

Public Relations Chair
Lisa Trice

Appetizers and Beverages

Looking Glass Falls

Take a trip through the Blue Ridge Mountains towards Brevard and you will be treated to splendid scenes of cascading waterfalls. One of the most breath-taking ones is Looking Glass Falls. There you will find the crystal clear waters of Looking Glass Creek plunging down sixty feet to the pools beneath. According to lore, when winter arrives and the falls freeze you can see your reflection in the results - a "looking-glass" provided by nature! For those who prefer visiting in the summer months, families can spend an enjoyable afternoon hiking through lush greenery of the Pisgah Forest to the falls. There they can relax and be refreshed by the gentle spray off the falls. An autumn trek will reward you with foliage of scarlet, russet, and gold. Its brilliance is memorable. No matter what season you view the falls; its long hike is sure to bring hunger! In the pages to follow, find something to take along with you on your next trip.

Zucchini Rounds with Gorgonzola

10 small zucchini
½ pound chilled Gorgonzola or any blue cheese, shredded
2 pints cherry tomatoes, sliced thinly

1 teaspoon dried basil
⅓ cup Parmesan cheese, finely grated
Freshly ground black pepper to taste
Kosher salt to taste

- Preheat oven to 400°.
- Line baking sheet with parchment paper. Wash zucchini and slice into ½-inch rounds. With a melon baller, scoop out center of each slice, leaving the bottom of each intact.
- Place ½ teaspoon Gorgonzola on each zucchini round. Place a slice of tomato on each round; top with a little basil and sprinkle with Parmesan cheese, pepper and salt.
- Place on baking sheet and bake 5 to 7 minutes. The cheese should be melted but not browned.
- Serve immediately.

Serves 40

Note: These may be prepared several hours ahead. Keep refrigerated, then bake at the last minute.

Caramelized Onion Dip

1 large red onion, quartered, thinly sliced
1 tablespoon unsalted butter
1 tablespoon peanut oil
½ cup sour cream
½ cup mayonnaise

¼ teaspoon salt
¼ teaspoon cayenne pepper
1 teaspoon red pepper flakes
⅛ teaspoon hot sauce

- Sauté onion in butter and oil 20 minutes or until golden brown and caramelized.
- Cool and combine with sour cream, mayonnaise, salt, cayenne, red pepper and hot sauce. Mix well and chill for at least 1 hour.
- Serve with crackers.

Serves 6

Marinated Vidalia Onions

---

6   large Vidalia onions
2   cups boiling water
1   cup sugar

½   cup cider vinegar
1-1½   cups mayonnaise
2   teaspoons celery seed

- Slice onions very thin. Separate into rings and place in shallow, covered container.
- Combine water, sugar and vinegar; stir to dissolve sugar. Pour hot mixture over onions.
- Cover and leave on kitchen counter overnight. On the next day, drain very well, squeezing out excess moisture.
- Add 1 cup mayonnaise and celery seed. Toss to coat well. Add up to ½ cup more mayonnaise, if needed. Chill several hours or overnight. Serve with saltines or any crackers. Will keep in refrigerator for up to one week.

Makes 5 to 6 cups

Vidalia Onion Dip

---

1   cup mayonnaise
1   cup sharp Cheddar cheese, grated
1   cup chopped Vidalia onion

¼   teaspoon hot sauce to taste
¼   teaspoon Worcestershire sauce to taste

- Preheat oven to 350°.
- Mix mayonnaise, cheese, onion, hot sauce and Worcestershire and pour into medium casserole dish.
- Bake 20 to 30 minutes or until golden brown on top.
- Serve warm with crackers or bagel chips.

Makes 3 cups

Date Nut Spread

2   (8-ounce) packages cream cheese, softened
2   tablespoons honey

¾   cup chopped dates
¾   cup chopped walnuts

- Combine cream cheese, honey, dates and walnuts until well mixed.
- Serve with crackers or on bagels.

Makes 3 cups

Reuben Dip

1   cup sauerkraut, rinsed and drained
½   pound corned beef, chopped
2   scallions, sliced
1   tablespoon butter
4   ounces cream cheese

1½ cups shredded Monterey Jack cheese
2   tablespoons catsup
2   teaspoons Dijon mustard
¼   teaspoon black pepper

- Preheat oven to 350°.
- Spoon sauerkraut into a small casserole dish to cover bottom. Gently stir in corned beef.

- Sauté scallions in butter until soft. Stir in cream cheese, Monterey Jack cheese, catsup, mustard and pepper. Cook over low heat until cheese melts.
- Spread cheese mixture over sauerkraut and corned beef.
- Bake for 10 to 15 minutes. Stir before serving. Serve on toasted rye bread.

Makes 5 cups

Hot Artichoke Spread

1	(14-ounce) can artichoke hearts, drained and chopped	4	drops Worcestershire sauce
1	cup mayonnaise	3	drops hot sauce
1	cup Parmesan cheese	1	(6½-ounce) can minced clams, drained
½	teaspoon garlic powder		Paprika for garnish

- Preheat oven to 350°.

- In a baking dish, combine artichoke hearts, mayonnaise, Parmesan cheese, garlic powder, Worcestershire, hot sauce and clams; mix well.

- Bake 20 minutes. Remove from oven and sprinkle paprika over top for garnish.

- Serve with crackers.

Serves 8 to 10

Spinach Artichoke Dip

2	(6½-ounce) jars marinated artichoke hearts, coarsely chopped	1	cup Parmesan cheese
1	(10-ounce) package frozen chopped spinach, thawed and drained	2½	cups Monterey Jack cheese, divided
1	cup mayonnaise	1	clove garlic, minced

- Preheat oven to 350°.

- In a medium bowl, combine artichoke hearts, spinach, mayonnaise, Parmesan cheese, 2 cups Monterey Jack cheese and garlic. Mix well.

- Place in baking dish and sprinkle remaining Monterey Jack cheese on top.

- Bake 15 minutes or until cheese is browned.

- Serve with your favorite crackers.

Serves 12

Avocado Crabmeat Spread

1	ripe avocado, peeled, seeded and mashed	1	teaspoon prepared mustard
1	tablespoon lemon juice	¼	teaspoon salt
2	tablespoons mayonnaise	¼	teaspoon hot sauce
2	tablespoons sour cream	6	ounces fresh crabmeat
2	tablespoons instant minced onion	4	ounces cream cheese, softened
1½	teaspoons lemon pepper	2	cherry tomatoes, halved
2	teaspoons chopped dill	1	red onion, chopped (optional)

- Combine avocado and lemon juice in a large bowl. Add mayonnaise, sour cream, onion, lemon pepper, dill, mustard, salt and hot sauce.
- Drain crabmeat thoroughly. Combine with cream cheese and fold into avocado mixture.
- Place in a decorative container. Garnish with tomatoes or red onion, if desired.
- Chill at least 2 hours prior to serving.

Serves 6 to 8

Smoked Oyster Pâté

2	(8-ounce) packages cream cheese, softened	¼	teaspoon onion salt
½	cup sliced ripe olives	1	(4-ounce) can smoked oysters, drained
½	cup chopped celery	½	cup chopped pecans or walnuts
1	tablespoon finely chopped onion		

- Combine cream cheese, olives, celery, onion and onion salt and mix well.
- Chop oysters into small pieces and add to cream cheese mixture.
- Shape into mound; cover with chopped nuts.
- Chill. Serve with plain crackers.

Serves 10

Layered Shrimp Dip

1½ pounds shrimp, cooked and peeled
1 (8-ounce) package cream cheese, softened
2 tablespoons sour cream
2 teaspoons Worcestershire sauce
1 teaspoon fresh lemon juice
½ teaspoon ground red pepper
1 clove garlic, minced

1 (12-ounce) bottle chili sauce
½ cup chopped onion
¾ cup sliced ripe olives
1 small bell pepper, finely chopped
2 cups shredded mozzarella cheese
Corn chips, tortilla chips or crackers

- Chop shrimp and set aside.
- In medium bowl, stir together cream cheese and sour cream. Stir in Worcestershire, lemon juice, red pepper and garlic.
- Spread mixture into bottom of 8-inch round serving dish. Layer chili sauce, onion, shrimp, olives, bell pepper and cheese on top.
- Serve with corn chips, tortilla chips or crackers.

Serves 10 to 12

Special Cheese Spread

1½ cups grated Cheddar cheese
1 cup chopped olives
½ cup mayonnaise

½ teaspoon curry powder
6 English muffins, halved

- Preheat oven to 350°.
- Mix cheese, olives, mayonnaise and curry until well blended. Spread onto English muffin halves and place on baking sheet.
- Bake 10 to 15 minutes or until bubbly and golden.
- Serve these with a bowl of soup in the winter, a simple salad in the summer or as a hearty appetizer anytime.

Serves 12

Broiled Cumin Shrimp

1   stick unsalted butter
2   teaspoons turmeric
1½ teaspoons ground cumin
1   teaspoon ground coriander

1½ teaspoons salt
     Juice of 2 lemons
2   pounds large shrimp, peeled and deveined

- Preheat oven broiler.

- Melt butter in a saucepan. Stir in turmeric, cumin, coriander, salt and lemon juice.

- Arrange shrimp in a single layer in shallow pan. Spread butter mixture over shrimp.

- Broil under high heat until shrimp are glazed and golden brown, about 8 minutes. Skewer with toothpicks and serve immediately.

Serves 12

Shrimp Olive Canapés

5   ounces freshly cooked or canned shrimp, diced
¼   cup diced black olives
1   (12-ounce) carton cream-style cottage cheese, drained

1   tablespoon lemon juice
¼   cup mayonnaise
2   green onions, minced
     Salt and pepper to taste

- In a medium bowl, blend shrimp, olives, cottage cheese, lemon juice, mayonnaise, green onions, salt and pepper. Chill 8 hours or overnight.

- Good as a spread for tea sandwiches or to serve with crackers or bagels.

Makes 4½ cups

On any given weekend in most Southern towns, you will find there is always at least one home on the street with cars filling their driveway and enticing aromas filling the air. Don't worry that your neighbors are opening a restaurant at home. Most likely, they are carrying out a solid tradition in our area — the Supper Club!

Supper Clubs are a wonderful way to try new foods, visit with old friends, and make new friends. They provide an excellent opportunity to experiment with new dishes or bring out your favorite recipes. As you turn these pages, you are sure to find delightful recipes that are sure to make your next gathering a success.

Tarragon Marinated Shrimp

2   pounds large shrimp, cooked, peeled and deveined
1⅓ cups olive oil
⅔   cup tarragon vinegar
1   large onion, chopped
1   clove garlic, minced
3   tablespoons Dijon mustard

2   tablespoons prepared horseradish
1   tablespoon thyme
½   teaspoon salt
¼   teaspoon black pepper
¼   teaspoon paprika

- Place cooked, peeled and deveined shrimp in a large glass bowl and set aside.
- Place oil, vinegar, onion, garlic, mustard, horseradish, thyme, salt, pepper and paprika into food processor or blender and blend until onion is minced. Pour marinade over shrimp.
- Cover and chill at least 1 day or up to 2 days.
- Drain and discard marinade. Serve shrimp with decorative picks.

Serves 8 to 12

Shrimp Butter

3   (4½-ounce) cans shrimp, drained, or 12 to 15 ounces
     fresh cooked shrimp
4   tablespoons mayonnaise
2   tablespoons minced onion
     Juice of 1 lemon

1½ sticks margarine, softened
1   (8-ounce) package cream cheese, softened
     Salt to taste
     Hot sauce to taste

- Chop shrimp very fine and set aside.
- In a medium bowl, combine mayonnaise, onion, lemon juice, margarine, cream cheese, salt and hot sauce. Beat with electric mixer until light and fluffy.
- Shape into mound or put into a mold. Chill several hours.
- Serve with Melba rounds or any bland cracker.

Makes 3 cups

Smoked Salmon Pizza

1 (13.8-ounce) can refrigerated pizza dough, or homemade pizza dough (see page 60)
  Olive oil
1 red onion, thinly sliced

¼ cup Dill Cream (see accompanying recipe)
  Cold smoked salmon, thinly sliced
  Chopped chives
  Caviar

- Preheat oven to 450°.
- Flatten dough with your fingers to make a 12-inch circle, thicker around the outer rim.
- Place crust on baking sheet or hot pizza stone. Brush with olive oil. Top generously with red onion.
- Bake 5 to 6 minutes or until golden brown.
- Spread Dill Cream over onions. Top with a layer of smoked salmon. Cut with a large knife.
- Garnish with chopped chives and caviar. Serve immediately.

Dill Cream

2 cups sour cream

3 tablespoons chopped fresh dill

2 tablespoons finely chopped shallots

3 tablespoons (or more) lemon juice

Salt and pepper to taste

- In a small bowl, combine sour cream, dill, shallots and lemon juice and mix well. Season with salt and pepper.

- Cover and chill.

Makes 2½ cups

Marinated Mushrooms

1 pound fresh mushrooms, washed and dried
1 (0.7-ounce) envelope Italian salad dressing mix

½ cup salad oil
½ cup cider vinegar
2-3 green onions, chopped

- Remove and discard stems from mushrooms. Mix together dressing mix, oil, vinegar and onion. Pour over mushrooms and toss. Marinate 24 hours, stirring occasionally.

Serves 6

Crisp Tortilla Strips

2 (7-inch) corn tortillas

2½ cups corn oil

- Cut tortillas into ¼-inch wide strips.

- In a heavy 3-quart saucepan, heat 2½ cups corn oil over medium heat to 375°. Carefully add tortilla strips, half at a time.

- Fry, turning once, 2 minutes or until lightly browned and crisp.

- Drain on paper towels.

Fresh Corn Salsa

6 ears fresh white corn (yellow corn or frozen may be used)

1 (15-ounce) can black beans, rinsed and drained

2 jalapeño peppers, finely chopped

1 yellow bell pepper, chopped

1 green bell pepper, chopped

1 cup cilantro, minced

2 cloves garlic, minced

¼ cup lime juice

¼ cup olive oil

Salt and pepper to taste

- If using fresh corn, husk corn and cut kernels off cob.

- In a large bowl, mix the corn with the beans, jalapeños, bell peppers, cilantro, garlic, lime juice, oil, salt and pepper.

- Serve with tortilla chips.

Makes 6 cups

Mexican Roll-Ups

2 (8-ounce) packages cream cheese, softened

1 (1 ounce) envelope Ranch-style dressing mix

4 ounces mild green chile peppers, drained

1 (4-ounce) jar diced pimientos, drained

1 (4¼-ounce) can chopped black olives, drained

1 bunch green onions, chopped

7-8 (10-inch) flour tortillas or floured flatbread

- Mix cream cheese and ranch dressing. Combine peppers, pimiento, olives and onion. Mix vegetable mixture with cream cheese mixture.

- Spread on tortillas. Roll up jelly roll style and wrap in plastic wrap. Chill overnight.

- Cut into pinwheels.

Makes 10 to 12 dozen pinwheels

Mushroom Turnovers

Dough

1   (8-ounce) package cream cheese, softened   1½ cups flour
½   cup butter

- Combine cream cheese and butter; mix well. Add flour and blend until smooth. Chill 30 minutes.
- Roll dough to ⅛-inch thickness and cut into 2 to 3-inch rounds.

Filling

1   large onion, finely chopped   ½   teaspoon salt
8   ounces fresh mushrooms, finely chopped   2   tablespoons flour
3   tablespoons butter   ¼   cup sweet or sour cream

- Preheat oven to 450°. Brown onion and mushrooms in butter. Add salt and sprinkle with flour. Stir in cream and cook until thick. Chill until cool.
- Place 1 teaspoon filling on each round and fold dough in half. Press edges with a fork and prick top.
- Bake approximately 15 minutes.

Makes 2 dozen

Petites Pissaladières

Miniature Onion Tartlets

Pastry squares can be baked 1 day ahead, cooled completely, and kept in an airtight container at room temperature. Reheat in a 350° oven 6 minutes before adding toppings.

Onion mixture can be made 1 day ahead and chilled, covered. Reheat over moderate heat, stirring, until heated through, about 10 minutes.

1 frozen puff pastry sheet (from a 17.3-ounce package), thawed

Flour

3 tablespoons olive oil, divided

1 large onion, halved lengthwise and cut crosswise into ⅛-inch thick slices

½ teaspoon salt

¼ teaspoon black pepper

3-4 flat anchovy fillets, patted dry and finely chopped

2 teaspoons chopped fresh thyme, divided

¼ cup kalamata or other brine-cured black olives, pitted and very thinly sliced lengthwise

- Preheat oven to 400°.

- Roll out puff pasty on a lightly floured surface into a 12½-inch square, then trim edges to form a 12-inch square. Prick sheet all over with a fork. Cut into 36 (2-inch) squares and transfer to two large, buttered baking sheets, arranging about 2 inches apart.

- Bake in upper and lower thirds of oven, switching position of pans halfway through baking, until puffed and golden, 12 to 15 minutes total. Transfer squares to a rack and cool until just warm.

- While pastry is baking, heat 2 tablespoons oil in a 12-inch skillet over moderate heat until hot but not smoking. Cook onion with salt and pepper, stirring occasionally, until golden brown, about 15 to 20 minutes. Stir in anchovies (to taste) and 1 teaspoon thyme and keep warm, covered.

- Lightly brush tops of pastry squares with remaining tablespoon oil. Make a small indention in center of each square with your finger, then top each with 1 teaspoon onion mixture and a few olive slivers. Sprinkle squares with remaining thyme.

Makes 36 tartlets

Variation: Sun-dried tomatoes packed in oil and finely chopped can be substituted for the anchovies.

Bruschetta with Gorgonzola and Peaches

4	ripe peaches	Garlic Toasts (see accompanying recipe)
1	pound Gorgonzola cheese	½ cup olive oil

- Preheat oven broiler.
- Peel peaches and split in half vertically. Twist the halves in opposite directions to pull apart. Slice into ¼-inch slices.
- Spread cheese evenly over Garlic Toasts.
- Place peaches on top of cheese. Drizzle with oil and broil until peaches are hot and soft, about 1 to 2 minutes.
- Serve immediately.

Makes 2 dozen

Garlic Toasts

1 loaf baguette bread

½ cup olive oil

4-6 cloves garlic, crushed

Dash paprika

- Preheat oven to 300°.

- Cut bread into ¼ to ½-inch thick slices.

- In a small bowl, blend oil, garlic and paprika. Brush each slice of bread with mixture on both sides.

- Bake on cookie sheet about 25 to 30 minutes, or until crisp and golden.

Caper and Olive Bruschetta

8-10	plum tomatoes	
½	teaspoon kosher salt	
½	cup kalamata olives, pitted and diced	
3	cloves garlic, pressed	
2	tablespoons extra virgin olive oil	
2	tablespoons balsamic vinegar	

3	tablespoons capers, coarsely chopped
2	tablespoons chopped fresh basil
½	teaspoon sugar
½	teaspoon black pepper
	Garlic Toasts (see accompanying recipe)

- Dice tomatoes and sprinkle with salt. Let stand on paper towels or in a colander for 1 hour.
- Combine tomatoes, olives, garlic, oil, vinegar, capers, basil, sugar and pepper. Chill 1 hour.
- Serve on Garlic Toasts.

Makes 3 cups

Hummus

Hummus can be flavored by adding one of the following:

(1)Hot sauce and red pepper flakes to taste (2) Cumin (3) Chopped sun-dried tomatoes (packed in oil) (4) Sliced black olives and toasted pine nuts

2   (19-ounce) cans chickpeas, rinsed and drained
3   tablespoons tahini paste (sesame seed paste)
½   cup lemon juice
1   tablespoon kosher salt to taste

Freshly ground black pepper to taste
4   medium cloves garlic
¼-½ cup olive oil
Crushed red pepper (optional)
Toasted pita bread wedges or pita chips

- Put chickpeas, tahini paste, lemon juice, salt and pepper in food processor fitted with metal blade. Crush garlic in a press and add to bowl.
- Purée, scraping down sides occasionally, until hummus is blended.
- Add olive oil slowly (or a combination of oil and water) to thin hummus to desired consistency and transfer hummus to a serving bowl.
- Serve at room temperature with toasted pita triangles or raw vegetables.

Makes about 4 cups

Spinach and Artichokes in Puff Pastry

1	(10-ounce) package frozen spinach, thawed	1	teaspoon garlic powder
1	(14-ounce) can artichoke hearts, drained and chopped	½	teaspoon black pepper
½	cup mayonnaise	1	(17.3-ounce) package frozen puff pastry
½	cup Parmesan cheese		Flour
1	teaspoon onion powder		

- Drain spinach well, pressing between layers of paper towels or squeezing out as much liquid as possible. Stir together spinach, artichoke hearts, mayonnaise, Parmesan cheese, onion powder, garlic powder, and pepper.

- Thaw puff pastry at room temperature for 30 minutes. Unfold and place on a lightly floured surface. Cover with plastic wrap and roll out slightly. Spread ¼ spinach mixture on pastry, leaving ½-inch border. Roll up pastry in jelly roll style. Press to seal seams and wrap in heavy duty plastic wrap. Repeat procedure with remaining pastry and spinach mixture. Freeze 30 minutes. Slice into ½-inch rounds. Bake at 400° for 20 minutes or until golden brown.

Makes 4 dozen squares

Phyllo Triangles with Curried Walnut Chicken

2½ pounds whole chicken breasts
1 pound plus 2 tablespoons unsalted butter, melted, divided
2½ tablespoons all-purpose flour
1½ teaspoons curry powder

1 cup milk
½ teaspoon kosher salt
½ cup chopped toasted walnuts
1 pound phyllo pastry

- Preheat oven to 375°.

- Arrange chicken breasts in a roasting pan and cook until juices run clear when pierced with a knife, about 45 minutes. Let cool.

- Remove skin and bones and discard. Cut meat into small pieces. Set aside.

- Heat 2 tablespoons butter in small pan. Add flour and curry powder and cook over low heat, stirring occasionally, about 2 minutes. Add milk and whisk until mixture thickens. Add salt. Stir in walnuts and chicken. Set aside to cool completely.

- To prepare the triangles, place one phyllo sheet on a flat surface and brush with melted butter. Top with 2 more sheets, buttering each layer. Cut the combined sheets in half crosswise. Then cut each half lengthwise into 2½-inch wide strips. Spoon filling onto center of the end of each strip and form a triangle by folding the lower right-hand corner to the opposite, as you would a flag. Continue folding to the end of the strip. Repeat with remaining phyllo and filling.

- Preheat oven to 375°. Line 2 baking sheets with parchment paper. Working in batches, place triangles on baking sheets, brushing them with melted butter and bake until golden brown, about 7 to 10 minutes.

- Filled triangles may be prepared ahead of time and refrigerated, unbaked, up to 2 days or frozen immediately. Do not thaw frozen triangles before baking.

Makes about 2 dozen

Chutney Cheese Balls

3 (8-ounce) packages cream cheese,
   softened
1 cup sour cream
1 cup chopped raisins
1 cup chopped salted peanuts
8 slices bacon, cooked until crisp and
   crumbled

½ cup chopped green onions
4 teaspoons curry powder
   Chutney
   Flaked coconut
   Fresh parsley, finely chopped

- Mix cream cheese, sour cream, raisins, peanuts, bacon, green onion and curry powder in a bowl. Shape mixture into 2 balls and wrap each in plastic wrap. Chill until firm.
- Unwrap and place on serving plates. Top with chutney, coconut and parsley.
- Serve with crackers.

Serves 20 to 30

The Chutney Cheese Balls may be made ahead and frozen up to 3 months. Thaw for 2 to 3 hours before topping with chutney, coconut and parsley.

Cheese Puffs

2 egg whites, stiffly beaten
1 (3-ounce) package cream cheese
¼ pound extra sharp Cheddar cheese

1 stick butter
1 loaf unsliced French bread

- Slice bread into 1-inch cubes. Melt butter and cheese in double boiler. Stir vigorously after melting until consistency of rarebit.
- Remove from heat and fold in egg whites. Spear bread cubes with fondue forks or toothpicks and dip in cheese mixture. Shake off excess. Place on cookie sheets lined with wax paper that has been sprayed with nonstick cooking spray. Chill overnight in freezer.
- Defrost 30 minutes. Heat oven to 400° and bake 10 to 12 minutes or until golden.
- Can be stored in plastic bag after being frozen for future use.

Makes 3 dozen

Blue Cheese Spread with Walnuts

12 walnut halves
2 (8-ounce) packages cream cheese, softened
5 ounces blue cheese (Roquefort, Gorgonzola or Stilton), at room temperature

1 tablespoon cognac
Salt and freshly ground pepper
1 bunch fresh chives, finely chopped

- Grate walnuts.
- Combine cream cheese and blue cheese, blending together with a fork. Add cognac, salt and pepper to taste. When mixture is smooth, add walnuts and chives. Mix well.
- Spoon into serving bowl and arrange with crackers, or spread on your favorite toasted bread or fresh vegetables.

Serves 8

Crunchy Fruit Dip

1 (8-ounce) package cream cheese, softened
¼ cup brown sugar
¾ cup sugar

1 teaspoon vanilla extract
4 toffee candy bars, crushed

- Blend cream cheese with both sugars and vanilla. Stir in crushed toffee candy bars. Keep refrigerated until serving. Serve with apples or preferred fruit.

Makes 2½ cups

Pesto Cheese Spread

½   pound unsalted butter, cut into pieces
12   ounces feta cheese, cut into pieces
1   (8-ounce) package cream cheese, cut into pieces
2   cloves garlic
1   shallot, minced

2-4   tablespoons vermouth
     White pepper
½   cup pine nuts, toasted
1   cup minced sun-dried tomatoes
1   cup pesto

- Combine butter, cheeses, garlic, shallots and vermouth. Blend well. Season with pepper.

- Oil a 4 to 5 cup straight-sided mold, bowl, or pâté dish. Line with plastic wrap. Layer ½-inch pine nuts, then sun-dried tomatoes, pesto and cheese mixture. Fold plastic over top. Press to compact. Refrigerate.

- To serve, remove from mold and invert onto serving plate. Let stand loosely covered at room temperature for about an hour to soften.

- Spread may be prepared five days in advance.

Serves 10 to 12

Baked Brie with Mango Chutney

---

1   (16-ounce) package bacon
1   (8-inch) round Brie cheese

1   cup mango chutney, chopped
½   cup slivered almonds

- Preheat oven to 350°.

- Cook bacon until crisp. Drain well and crumble.

- Place cheese in 10-inch quiche dish or pie plate.

- Spread chutney on top of cheese, leaving ½-inch margin around sides. Sprinkle with bacon and add almonds.

- Bake for about 25 minutes.

- Serve with crackers.

Serves 12 to 15

Baked Brie with Caramelized Apple Topping

1 large Granny Smith apple, peeled, cored and coarsely chopped (about 2 cups)
½ cup pecan pieces

⅓ cup packed brown sugar
2 tablespoons Kahlúa
1 (2-pound) round Brie, rind left on

- Preheat oven to 325°.
- Mix apple with pecans, brown sugar and Kahlúa. Set aside.
- Place Brie in shallow, oven-proof dish. Top with apple mixture. Bake 10 to 15 minutes or until topping is bubbly and cheese is softened.
- Serve with water crackers.

Serves 16 to 20

Hot Asparagus Canapés

20 slices thin white bread
3 ounces blue cheese
1 (8-ounce) package cream cheese

1 egg
1 can asparagus spears, drained well
½ pound butter, melted

- Preheat oven to 400°.
- Trim crusts and flatten bread slightly with rolling pin.
- Blend cheeses and egg. Spread evenly over bread.
- Roll diagonally an asparagus spear in each flattened bread slice and fasten with a toothpick.
- Baste with melted butter and place on cookie sheet; refrigerate or freeze.
- Bake for 15 minutes or until brown.
- If frozen, thaw before baking.

Serves 20

Cocktail Meatballs

1½ pounds ground beef
¼ cup seasoned bread crumbs
1 medium onion, chopped
2 teaspoons prepared horseradish
2 cloves garlic, crushed
¾ cup tomato juice
2 teaspoons salt
¼ teaspoon black pepper
2 tablespoons butter

1 medium onion, chopped
2 tablespoons flour
1½ cups beef broth
½ cup dry red wine
2 tablespoons brown sugar
2 tablespoons catsup
1 tablespoon lemon juice
3 gingersnaps, crumbled

- Preheat oven to 450°.

- Combine ground beef, bread crumbs, onion, horseradish, garlic, tomato juice, salt and pepper. Shape into 1-inch balls and place in baking dish.

- Bake 20 minutes. Drain

- Heat butter in large skillet; sauté onion until tender. Blend in flour; gradually add beef broth, stirring constantly. Add wine, brown sugar, catsup, lemon juice and gingersnaps.

- Cook over low heat 15 minutes; add meatballs and simmer 5 minutes.

Makes about 4 dozen

Spicy Cheese Twists

---

1   **(17.3-ounce) package frozen puff pastry, thawed**   **Cayenne pepper to taste**
¾   **cup grated Parmesan cheese (not powdered), divided**

- Preheat oven to 350°.
- Roll out puff pastry dough into a rectangle 20 x 24 inches. Sprinkle half of Parmesan cheese evenly over dough and gently press cheese into dough with a rolling pin.
- Fold dough in half crosswise, roll it out again to 20 x 24 inches and sprinkle with remaining cheese. Sprinkle lightly with cayenne pepper to taste.
- Using a sharp thin knife, cut dough into ⅓-inch strips. Take each strip by its end and twist until evenly corkscrewed. Lay twists of dough on ungreased baking sheet, arranged so they are just touching; this will prevent untwisting.
- Set baking sheet in middle of oven and bake until straws are crisp, puffed and browned, 15 to 20 minutes.
- Remove from oven, cool for 5 minutes, then cut apart with a sharp knife. Finish cooling straws on a rack, then store in airtight tin or plastic bag until serving time.
- These will stay fresh for about a week.

20 straws

Lillie's Cheese Straws

1	pound aged sharp Cheddar cheese, grated	⅛	teaspoon cayenne pepper
2	cups flour, sifted	1	stick margarine
		1	teaspoon salt

- Preheat oven to 425°.
- Mix cheese, flour, cayenne pepper, margarine and salt until well blended. Roll out dough and cut into strips.
- Roll edges with a small rolling wheel to make them pretty.
- Bake 10 to 12 minutes or until crisp and golden brown.

Serves 30

Lillie's Cheese Straws placed in a decorative tin makes a nice gift for any occasion.

Bridge Party Popcorn Mix

6	cups popped popcorn	1	cup brown sugar
2	cups corn cereal squares	½	cup margarine or butter
2	cups rice cereal squares	¼	cup light corn syrup
2	cups wheat cereal squares	1	teaspoon vanilla extract
2	cups mixed nuts	¼	teaspoon baking soda
1	cup pecans		

- Preheat oven to 250°.
- Combine popcorn, cereals, mixed nuts and pecans. Transfer to a greased roasting pan.
- In a heavy 2 to 3-quart saucepan, combine sugar, margarine and corn syrup. Cook to boiling. Remove from heat, stir in vanilla and baking soda. Pour sugar mixture over popcorn mix.
- Bake 1 hour. Cool.

Makes 14 cups

Whether it is a ladies group that meets in the morning or a couples' group that gathers in the evening, bridge clubs have always provided special times for their members and that unique opportunity to mix cards and conversation. If you are searching for a treat to nibble on during a hand, here is a recipe sure to tempt even the most devoted bridge player away from the card table!

Cinnamon Nuts

1 egg white

1 tablespoon water

1 pound pecan halves

1 cup sugar

1 teaspoon ground cinnamon

1 teaspoon salt

• Preheat oven to 250°.

• Beat egg white and water together until frothy. Add pecans and stir until completely coated.

• In a separate bowl, combine sugar, cinnamon and salt. Mix with nuts, stirring until coated.

• Spread coated nuts on flat baking sheet. Bake for 1 hour, stirring every 15 minutes.

Makes 4 cups

Spiced Pecans

1 tablespoon olive oil	½ teaspoon paprika
2 tablespoons butter	½ teaspoon garlic powder
1 tablespoon Worcestershire sauce	2 cups pecan halves
½ teaspoon hot sauce	1½ teaspoons coarse salt
¾ teaspoon ground cumin	

• Preheat oven to 325°.

• In a small saucepan, heat oil and butter over low heat. Add Worcestershire, hot sauce, cumin, paprika and garlic powder. Simmer 2 to 3 minutes to blend.

• Add pecans and toss to coat. Spread out on a baking sheet and bake 15 minutes, shaking occasionally.

• Toss hot nuts with salt.

Makes 2 cups

Hot Holiday Punch

1 cup sugar	2 quarts orange juice
1 cup water	1 quart cranberry juice cocktail
1 teaspoon whole cloves	¼ cup lemon juice
3 sticks cinnamon	

• In a large saucepan, simmer sugar, water, cloves and cinnamon sticks for 15 minutes.

• Strain cloves and cinnamon from pan. Add orange juice, cranberry juice cocktail and lemon juice.

• Heat but do not boil.

Makes 15 to 20 servings, 4 ounces each

Lynchburg Slush

2   cups water
⅓   cup sugar
1   (6-ounce) can frozen lemonade
     concentrate, thawed

½   cup Jack Daniel's Tennessee whiskey
1   liter ginger ale
     Lemon slices

Enjoy on a summer evening when entertaining with friends.

- Blend water, sugar, lemonade and whiskey until sugar dissolves. Freeze overnight.
- To serve, add frozen mixture to a 2-quart pitcher along with ginger ale and garnish with lemon slices.

Serves 8

Riverboat Wedding Punch

1   (12-ounce) can frozen orange juice
     concentrate, thawed
1   (12-ounce) can frozen lemonade
     concentrate, thawed
½   cup sugar

1   (1-ounce) bottle almond flavoring
     (or 2 tablespoons)
1   (1-ounce) bottle vanilla flavoring
2   (10-ounce) bottles ginger ale

- Mix orange juice and lemonade according to package directions. Stir in ½ cup sugar, almond and vanilla flavorings.
- Freeze, stirring every 30 minutes. Mixture will usually stay slushy and will not freeze solid.
- When ready to serve, pour ginger ale over frozen punch.

Serves 20

Spiced Tropical Tea Cooler

6 cups water, divided
6 orange-and-spice-flavored tea bags
1 large fresh mint sprig
1 (12-ounce) can frozen orange-peach-mango juice
  concentrate, thawed and undiluted

¼ cup sugar
  Ice cubes
1 medium orange for garnish
  Freshly chopped mint for garnish

- Bring 4 cups water to a boil. Place tea bags and whole mint sprig in a bowl; carefully add boiling water. Let steep 5 minutes. Remove tea bags and mint.

- Place remaining 2 cups water, juice concentrate and sugar into a large pitcher. Add hot tea; mix well. Refrigerate at least 2 hours or overnight.

- To serve, pour tea mixture into ice-filled glasses. Score orange and cut into thin slices. Garnish ice tea with orange slices and mint, if desired.

Serves 6

Peach Daiquiris

2 (6-ounce) cans frozen lemonade concentrate, thawed
2 ounces peach-flavored liqueur
4 ounces spiced rum
  Handful fresh or frozen peaches, peeled and sliced

1-2 cups ice cubes
  Mint leaves for garnish
  Lemon slice for garnish

- Place lemonade, peach liqueur, rum, peaches and ice in blender. Crush/blend to desired consistency.

- Serve in chilled glasses. Garnish with lemon or mint leaf, if desired.

Serves 4

Mango Margaritas

1   (26-ounce) jar sliced mangoes, undrained
   Colored decorator sugar
1   (6-ounce) can frozen limeade concentrate, thawed
1   cup gold tequila

½   cup Triple Sec or Cointreau
¼   cup Grand Marnier
   Crushed ice

- Spoon 3 tablespoons mango liquid into a saucer; pour mangoes and remaining liquid into container of an electric blender.
- Place sugar in a saucer; dip rims of glasses into mango liquid, and then sugar. Set aside.
- Add limeade concentrate with tequila, Triple Sec and Grand Marnier into blender; process until smooth, stopping once to scrape down sides.
- Pour half of mixture into a small pitcher and set aside.
- Add ice to remaining mixture in blender to bring it up to 5-cup level; process until slushy, stopping to scrape down sides. Pour into prepared glasses; repeat with remaining mango mixture and ice.
- Serve immediately.

Makes 10 cups

Cranberry Shower Punch

1   quart cranberry juice cocktail
1   (6-ounce) can frozen orange juice concentrate, thawed and undiluted
1   (6-ounce) frozen lemonade concentrate, thawed and undiluted

2   cups water
1¾ cups ginger ale
   Orange slices for garnish

- Combine cranberry juice cocktail, orange juice concentrate, lemonade concentrate. Add water, chill well.
- Just before serving, pour juice mixture over ice. Gently stir in ginger ale. Garnish with orange slices.

Makes 2½ quarts

Coffee Punch

Excellent for bridal tea

2	cups milk	1	cup heavy cream, whipped
2	quarts strong brewed coffee, cooled	1	quart ice cream: vanilla, chocolate or coffee-flavored
2½	teaspoons vanilla extract		Nutmeg
½	cup sugar		

- Mix milk, coffee, vanilla and sugar in a pitcher and chill for several hours.
- To serve, place ice cream in a punch bowl, break into chunks with a spoon and pour coffee-milk mixture over it. Cover top with dollops of whipped cream. Sprinkle with nutmeg.
- Serve in punch cups.

Serves 10

Variation: For a spiked coffee punch, stir in 2 cups Kahlúa before adding whipped cream on top.

Mocha Malted Shake

1	pint chocolate ice cream	5	tablespoons malted milk powder
¾	cup strong brewed coffee, chilled		

- Blend ice cream, coffee and milk powder in a blender until smooth.

Makes about 3 cups

Variation: To save time, 4 teaspoons instant coffee and ¾ cup cold water can be substituted for freshly brewed coffee.

Peach Raspberry Smoothie

¾ pound ripe peaches, pitted and cut into ½-inch wedges
1 cup water
1 cup (8 ounces) fresh raspberries

¼ cup sugar
⅛ teaspoon almond extract

- Freeze peaches in 1 layer in a large sealed plastic bag until frozen, about 4 hours.
- Blend peaches with water, raspberries, sugar and almond extract in a blender until smooth. Thin with more water if necessary.

Makes about 3½ cups

Strawberry Banana Smoothie

1 pound strawberries (about 1 quart), trimmed and halved
1 ripe banana
1 cup ice cubes

½ cup silken tofu
½ cup orange juice
2 tablespoons sugar

- Blend strawberries, banana, ice, tofu, orange juice and sugar in a blender until smooth.

Makes about 4 cups

Tropical Smoothie

1   (1-pound) ripe papaya, peeled, seeded and chopped (2 cups)

1   ripe mango, peeled, pitted and chopped (2 cups)

5   tablespoons fresh lime juice

⅓   cup water

2   tablespoons peeled, chopped fresh ginger

1   cup coconut sorbet

1   cup ice cubes

- Blend together papaya, mango, lime juice, water and ginger in a blender until smooth.

- Add sorbet and ice and blend until smooth.

Makes about 4 cups

Honeydew Cucumber Smoothie

1½ pounds ripe honeydew melon

1   medium cucumber

1   cup lemon yogurt

2   tablespoons chopped fresh mint

1-2 teaspoons sugar

- Remove seeds and rind from honeydew and cut flesh into ½-inch pieces to produce 3 cups.

- Freeze honeydew in 1 layer in a large, sealed plastic bag until frozen, about 4 hours.

- Peel and chop cucumber (1 cup).

- Blend frozen honeydew with cucumber, yogurt, mint, and sugar (to taste) in a blender until smooth. Thin with water if necessary.

Makes about 4 cups

Breads and Brunch

Cove Creek Falls

The mountains of North Carolina entreat many to visit them.
Of particular attraction are the thousands of waterfalls that dot
the region. Whether long slip-streams etched across a rocky face or
coursing torrents pouring over sheer cliffs. These scenes appeal
to us to draw near. Cove Creek Falls provides a magnificent place
to camp near this natural spectacle. Pitch a tent…snuggle
into sleeping bags…draw your family near…

And listen…

Listen to the symphony of Cove Creek Falls coursing over rocks
and gurgling down stream. Smell the sweet aroma of night air mixed
with mist of the falls. See the sun rise on water that is glistening and
bright. And after you have replenished your senses, you'll need to
answer your appetite. Leaf through the next section and find
recipes that are sure to be a complement to your next adventure.

Bread and Butter Pickles

25-30	small to medium cucumbers	5	cups sugar
8	white onions	1	tablespoon mustard seed
½	cup salt	1	teaspoon celery seed
5	cups vinegar	1	teaspoon turmeric

- Slice cucumbers very thin and sprinkle with salt. Let stand 3 hours. Drain.
- Slice onions and combine with cucumbers in a large stockpot.
- In a large saucepan, combine vinegar, sugar, mustard seed, celery seed and turmeric. Bring to a boil.
- Pour mixture over drained cucumbers and onions in stockpot. Heat but do not boil. Pack pickles into hot, sterilized pint jars and seal.

Makes 12 pints

Pepper Jelly

¼	cup ground red hot pepper	1½	cups apple cider vinegar
¾	cup ground green bell pepper	1	(1¾-ounce) package powdered pectin
6½	cups sugar		

- In a large saucepan, mix red hot pepper, bell pepper, sugar and vinegar. Bring to a full rolling boil, stirring constantly, and boil 5 minutes.
- Remove from heat and cool 2 minutes; stir in pectin. Quickly skim off foam with a metal spoon. Ladle into hot, sterilized half-pint jars, leaving ¼-inch headspace. Wipe jar rims; adjust lids.
- Process in a boiling water bath for 10 minutes. Remove jars and cool on a wire rack until lids seal.

Makes 8 half-pints

Peach Chutney

4	quarts peeled and finely chopped fresh peaches	3	cups firmly packed brown sugar
1	cup chopped onion	¼	cup whole mustard seeds
1	cup raisins	2	tablespoons ground ginger
1	clove garlic, minced	2	teaspoons salt
1	hot red pepper	5	cups white vinegar (5% acidity)

- In a large Dutch oven, combine peaches, onion, raisins, garlic, red pepper, brown sugar, mustard seeds, ginger, salt and vinegar. Bring to a boil, stirring frequently. Reduce heat and simmer, uncovered, 2 hours or until thickened; stirring often.
- Quickly spoon chutney into hot, sterilized pint jars, leaving ¼-inch headspace; wipe jar rims and cover at once with metal lids and screw bands tightly. Process in boiling water bath 10 minutes. Remove jars and cool on a wire rack until lids are sealed.

Makes 6 pints

Pear Relish

10-12	medium pears, peeled, cored and ground	2	hot peppers, seeded and ground
5	green bell peppers, ground	2	cups cider vinegar
5	red bell peppers, ground	1	(1-pound) box light brown sugar
10	medium onions, ground	1	tablespoon salt

- Grind each ingredient separately; then combine in a large stockpot. Add brown sugar, vinegar and salt.
- Bring to a boil and cook 15 minutes. Ladle into hot sterilized jars; wipe jar rims and adjust metal lids and bands.

Makes 6 pints

Squash Pickles

cups thinly sliced squash
cups chopped thinly sliced onion
bell peppers, sliced
cups vinegar

3   cups sugar
2   teaspoons celery seed
2   teaspoons mustard seed
    Salt

- Sprinkle squash, onion and peppers with salt freely. Set 1 hour.
- Drain off liquid. Combine vinegar, sugar, celery seed and mustard seed. Bring to a full rolling boil. Add squash mixture and return to a full rolling boil. Pack pickles into hot, sterilized jars; wipe jar rims and seal with metal lids and bands.

Makes 6 pints

Pecan Pie Mini-Muffins

Vegetable oil
Floured baking spray
1   cup firmly packed brown sugar
1/2 cup all-purpose flour

1   cup chopped pecans
2/3 cup butter, do not substitute
2   eggs

- Preheat oven to 350°.
- Coat a mini-muffin pan with vegetable oil and floured baking spray. In a bowl, combine brown sugar, flour and pecans. Set aside.
- Melt butter and combine with eggs. Mix well. Stir into flour mixture until batter is just moistened.
- Fill mini-muffin cups 2/3 full with muffin mixture. Bake 12 to 15 minutes or until muffins are lightly browned and test done with a toothpick.
- Remove from oven and immediately turn out onto a wire rack to cool.

Makes about 2 1/2 dozen muffins

Homemade Granola

Orange Yogurt

2 pints plain yogurt

¼ cup raisins

¼ cup chopped walnuts

1½ teaspoons pure vanilla extract

¼ cup good quality honey

1 orange, zest grated

½-1 cup freshly squeezed orange juice

Orange, orange zest, raisins and walnuts for garnish (optional)

• Line a sieve with cheesecloth or paper towels and suspend over a bowl. Pour yogurt into sieve and allow to drain, refrigerated, 3 hours or overnight.

• Place thickened yogurt into medium bowl and stir in raisins, walnuts, vanilla, honey and orange zest. Thin with orange juice until desired consistency. Garnish with sections of orange, orange zest, raisins or walnuts and serve.

Serves 4

4	cups old-fashioned rolled oats	1	cup small diced dried figs
2	cups sweetened shredded coconut	1	cup dried cherries
2	cups sliced almonds	1	cup dried cranberries
¾	cup vegetable oil	1	cup roasted, unsalted cashews
½	cup good quality honey		Orange Yogurt (see accompanying recipe)
1½	cups diced dried apricots		

• Preheat oven to 350°.

• Toss oats, coconut and almonds together in a large bowl. Whisk together oil and honey in a small bowl. Pour liquids over oat mixture and stir with a wooden spoon until all oats and almonds are coated.

• Pour onto a 13 x 18 x 1-inch sheet pan. Bake, stirring occasionally with a spatula, until mixture turns a nice, even golden brown, about 45 minutes.

• Remove granola from oven and allow to cool, stirring occasionally. Add apricots, figs, cherries, cranberries and cashews. Store cooled granola in an airtight container. Serve with Orange Yogurt.

Makes 12 cups

Note: If you wish to make a smaller amount, the pan size must be decreased accordingly. For the original amount, the pan will be quite full, but don't be tempted to use 2 pans – your granola could burn by doing so. It is also recommended to stir every 10 to 15 minutes for even browning.

Lemon-Poppy Seed Biscotti

2   cups flour
1   cup sugar
¼   cup poppy seeds
1   teaspoon baking powder
½   teaspoon baking soda

¼   teaspoon salt
2   large eggs
2   large egg whites
3   tablespoons fresh lemon juice
1   tablespoon grated lemon zest

- Preheat oven to 325°.
- Lightly grease a large cookie sheet. Combine flour, sugar, poppy seeds, baking powder and baking soda. Whisk together salt, eggs, egg whites and lemon juice. Add to dry ingredients; mix well.
- Working on a lightly floured surface, turn out dough (will be sticky). Flour hand and shape dough into 2 equal logs, about 3 x 8-inches long.
- Place onto cookie sheet and bake 25 to 30 minutes or until firm to the touch.
- Remove from oven, leave on pan and cool 10 minutes. Slice crosswise into ½-inch slices. Lay on their sides on cookie sheets and return to oven 10 minutes. Remove to wire rack and cool. Store in airtight container to maintain crisp texture.

Makes 32 biscotti

Note: Great for dipping into coffee or tea.

Blueberry Muffins

2 cups unbleached all-purpose flour

1 tablespoon baking powder

½ teaspoon salt

1 large egg

1 cup sugar

4 tablespoons unsalted butter, melted and cooled slightly

1¼ cups sour cream

1½ cups frozen blueberries, preferably wild

- Adjust oven rack to middle position and preheat oven to 350°.

- Spray standard muffin pan with nonstick spray, or line with muffin cups.

- Whisk flour, baking powder and salt in a medium bowl until combined. Whisk egg in a separate medium bowl until well beaten and light-colored, about 20 seconds. Add sugar and whisk vigorously until thick and homogeneous, about 30 seconds; add melted butter in 2 or 3 additions, whisking to combine after each addition. Add sour cream in 2 additions, whisking just to combine.

- Add frozen berries to dry ingredients and gently toss just to combine. Add sour cream mixture and fold with rubber spatula until batter comes together and berries are evenly distributed, 25 to 30 seconds. (Small spots of flour may remain and batter will be thick, do not over mix.)

- Use standard ice cream scoop or large spoon to drop batter into muffin pan (batter will fill most of cup). Bake until light golden brown and toothpick or skewer inserted into center of muffin comes out clean, 25 to 30 minutes, rotating pan from front to back halfway through baking time. Invert muffins onto wire rack, stand muffins upright, and cool 5 minutes. Serve as is or use one of toppings below.

Cinnamon Sugar-Dipped Muffins

½ cup sugar

½ teaspoon ground cinnamon

4 tablespoons butter

- While muffins are cooling, mix sugar and cinnamon in a small bowl. Melt butter in a small saucepan. After baked muffins have cooled 5 minutes, dip each muffin in melted butter and then cinnamon-sugar mixture. Set muffins upright on wire rack.

Ginger- or Lemon-Glazed Muffins

1 teaspoon freshly grated ginger or lemon zest

¾ cup sugar, divided

¼ cup lemon juice

Blueberry Muffins continued

- While muffins are baking, mix ginger or lemon zest with ½ cup sugar in a small bowl. Bring lemon juice and ¼ cup sugar to simmer in a small saucepan over medium heat; stirring until mixture is thick and syrupy and reduced to about 4 tablespoons. After baked muffins have cooled 5 minutes, brush tops with glaze, then dip tops of muffins in lemon sugar or ginger sugar. Set muffins upright on wire rack.

Makes 12 muffins

Note: When making batter, be sure to whisk vigorously step 2 with egg and sugar; then fold carefully in step 3 with sour cream mixture. There should not be large pockets of flour in finished batter, but small occasional spots may remain.

Beach Bran Muffins

6	cups all-bran cereal, divided		5	cups all-purpose flour
2	cups boiling water		5	teaspoons baking soda
1	cup oil		2	teaspoons salt
4	eggs, beaten		24	ounces apple butter
3	cups sugar		2	cups chopped walnuts (optional)
1	quart buttermilk		2	cups raisins (optional)

- Preheat oven to 400°.
- Pour boiling water over 2 cups bran. Add oil. Mix and let stand while assembling other ingredients.
- In a separate bowl, mix together eggs, sugar, buttermilk and remaining bran in that order.
- In a third bowl, sift flour with soda and salt. Combine all three mixtures; then stir in apple butter; then walnuts and raisins last. Bake in greased muffin pan at 400° 15 to 20 minutes.
- Mixture keeps 6 weeks in refrigerator. Muffins freeze well.

Makes 6 dozen muffins

Bran Surprise Muffins

Filling

1   (8-ounce) package cream cheese, softened
⅓   cup sugar

2   tablespoons all-purpose flour
1   teaspoon vanilla extract

- Mix together cream cheese, sugar, flour and vanilla until well blended. Keeps, refrigerated, 1 week.

Muffin Batter

2½ cups all-purpose flour
2   cups sugar
2½ teaspoons baking soda
1   teaspoon salt
1   tablespoon ground cinnamon
½   teaspoon freshly grated nutmeg

3½ cups raisin bran cereal
2   large eggs, lightly beaten
2   cups well shaken buttermilk
½   cup vegetable oil
½   cup raisins

- Place rack in middle position of oven and preheat oven to 400°. Line 24 (½-cup) muffin tins with paper liners.
- In a large bowl, sift together flour, sugar, baking soda, salt, cinnamon and nutmeg. Stir in cereal. Add eggs, buttermilk, oil and raisins, stirring just until combined well.
- Batter keeps, covered and chilled, 1 week.
- Spoon 1 heaping tablespoon batter into each tin and top with 2 teaspoons filling. Spoon 1 heaping tablespoon batter over filling, spreading to cover filling completely. Bake muffins 20 to 25 minutes, or until a tester comes out clean.

Makes 24 muffins

Banana-Praline Muffins

⅓ cup chopped pecans, toasted
3 tablespoons brown sugar
1 tablespoon light sour cream
3 ripe bananas
1 large egg

1½ cups pancake mix
½ cup granulated sugar
2 tablespoons vegetable oil
  Nonstick cooking spray
1 cup sweetened dried cranberries (optional)

- Preheat oven to 400°.
- Stir together pecans, brown sugar and sour cream. Set aside.
- Mash bananas in a medium bowl; add egg, pancake mix, sugar and oil and stir until mix is completely moistened.
- Place paper liners into muffin tins and coat cups with nonstick cooking spray.
- Stir cranberries into batter mixture, if desired. Spoon batter into muffin cups, filling ¾ full. Carefully spoon pecan mixture evenly in center of each muffin.
- Bake 18 to 20 minutes or until golden brown. Remove from oven and immediately turn out onto a wire rack to cool.

Makes 1 dozen

Honey Oatmeal Ricotta Muffins

1 egg
1 cup whole milk ricotta cheese
¾ cup honey
⅓ cup butter, softened
1¼ cups quick-cooking rolled oats, divided

2 tablespoons grated orange zest
½ teaspoon baking soda
1 cup self-rising flour
1 cup raisins
1 cup chopped walnuts

- Preheat oven to 375°.
- Beat egg and ricotta cheese; stir in honey and butter. Mix in 1 cup oats, orange zest and baking soda. Gradually stir in flour, add the raisins and walnuts; spoon into greased muffin tins.
- Sprinkle remaining oats over muffins. Bake 20 to 25 minutes or until done.

Makes 12 muffins

Carrot Spice Muffins

2 cups flour
2 cups light brown sugar
2 teaspoons baking powder
1 teaspoon salt
2 teaspoons ground cinnamon
1 teaspoon ground ginger
½ teaspoon cloves
¼ cup canola oil
½ cup applesauce
1 egg

1 egg white
2 teaspoons vanilla extract
2 (2½-ounce) jars strained carrot baby food
½ cup orange juice
4 ounces crushed pineapple with juice
Nonstick cooking spray
¾ cup loosely packed shredded coconut
½ cup confectioners' sugar (optional)
2 tablespoons lemon juice (optional)
Lemon zest (optional)

- Preheat oven to 350°.

- Mix together flour, brown sugar, baking powder, salt, cinnamon, ginger and cloves.

- Stir in oil, applesauce, eggs, vanilla, baby food, orange juice and pineapple; mix until well blended. Stir in coconut.

- Spray muffin pans and fill to top. Bake 20 to 25 minutes.

- A glaze can be prepared, if desired, by mixing confectioners' sugar with lemon juice and zest and spread on top of baked muffins.

Makes approximately 16 muffins

Cherry Coffee Cake

1 (3-ounce) package dried cherries (about ⅔ cup), chopped
½ cup hot water
½ teaspoon almond extract
1½ cups all-purpose flour
2 teaspoons baking powder
¼ teaspoon salt

1 cup plus 1 tablespoon sugar, divided
1 (8-ounce) carton vanilla low-fat yogurt
½ cup vegetable oil
1 large egg, lightly beaten
1 egg white, lightly beaten
¼ cup finely chopped pecans

- Combine cherries, hot water and almond extract; let stand 20 minutes.
- Drain cherries, and pat dry between layers of paper towels; set aside.
- Preheat oven to 350°.
- Combine flour, baking powder, salt and 1 cup sugar in a bowl; add yogurt, oil and eggs, stirring well. Fold in cherries. Pour batter into a greased and floured 9-inch round cake pan.
- Combine pecans and 1 tablespoon sugar; sprinkle over batter.
- Bake 35 minutes or until a wooden pick inserted in center comes out clean. Cool in pan on a wire rack 10 minutes; cut into wedges. Serve warm or at room temperature.

Makes 1 (9-inch) cake

New York-Style Crumb Cake

2   tablespoons canola oil

4   cups all-purpose flour, divided

½   cup granulated sugar

2½ teaspoons baking powder

½   teaspoon salt

1   large egg

½   cup milk

2   teaspoons pure vanilla extract

1   cup firmly packed light brown sugar

1½ teaspoons ground cinnamon

2   sticks unsalted butter, melted and cooled
    Confectioners' sugar for garnish

- Place rack in center of oven and preheat oven to 325°. Lightly brush a 13 x 9 x 2-inch baking pan with canola oil; dust with flour and tap to remove excess. Set aside.

- In a medium bowl, sift together 1½ cups flour, granulated sugar, baking powder and salt; set aside.

- In a separate bowl, whisk together egg, milk, 2 tablespoons canola oil and vanilla. Using a rubber spatula, fold dry ingredients into egg mixture. Spread batter evenly into prepared pan and set aside.

- In a medium bowl, combine remaining 2½ cups flour, brown sugar and cinnamon. Pour melted butter over flour mixture and toss with a rubber spatula until large crumbs form. Sprinkle crumbs over batter.

- Transfer pan to oven, and bake, rotating pan after 10 minutes. Continue baking until a cake tester comes out clean, about 10 more minutes.

- Transfer baking pan to wire rack to cool. Dust with confectioners' sugar. Using a serrated knife or bench scraper, cut into 3-inch squares. Store in an airtight container for up to 3 days.

Cranberry Coffee Cake

½ cup butter or margarine, softened

1 cup sugar

2 eggs

1 teaspoon baking soda

½ teaspoon salt

2 cups all-purpose flour

1 cup sour cream

1 teaspoon vanilla extract

½ cup chopped nuts

1 can whole cranberry sauce

- Preheat oven to 350°.

- Cream butter and sugar. Add unbeaten eggs, one at a time. Sift dry ingredients. Add alternately with sour cream to batter. Add vanilla and nuts.

- Pour ⅓ batter into greased and floured 10 x 4-inch tube pan or Bundt pan. Spread a layer of cranberry sauce over batter. Repeat, ending with layer of batter.

- Bake 55 to 60 minutes. Cool 10 to 15 minutes.

Glaze

¾ cup confectioners' sugar

1 tablespoon water or milk

½ teaspoon almond extract

- Combine confectioners' sugar, water and almond extract. Pour over cake.

Serves 12 to 15

Note: Freezes well. If milder cranberry flavor is desired, use ½ can of sauce.

Apple and Pecan Bread

---

1 cup sugar
1 (8-ounce) carton sour cream
2 eggs
2 teaspoons vanilla extract
2 cups all-purpose flour
2 teaspoons baking powder

½ teaspoon baking soda
1¼ cups tart apple, chopped
1 cup chopped pecans, divided
¼ cup butter
¼ cup brown sugar

- Preheat oven to 350°.
- Beat sugar, sour cream, eggs and vanilla for 2 minutes. Add dry ingredients. Stir in apple and ½ cup nuts. Pour into a 9 x 5 x 3-inch loaf pan. Press remaining nuts on top.
- Bake 1 hour. When done, bring butter and brown sugar to boil in a saucepan. Boil 1 minute. Pour over bread and serve.

Yield: 1 loaf

Blueberry Orange Cheese Bread

---

2 cups all-purpose flour
1 cup sugar
1 cup shredded sharp Cheddar cheese
1 tablespoon grated orange zest
1½ teaspoons baking powder
1½ teaspoons baking soda

1 teaspoon salt
¾ cup orange juice
2 tablespoons shortening
1 egg
1 cup blueberries

- Preheat oven to 350°.
- Mix flour, sugar, cheese, zest, baking powder, baking soda and salt. In a separate bowl, combine orange juice, shortening and egg.
- Combine flour mixture and egg mixture. Fold in berries. Pour into a well-greased 9 x 5 x 3-inch loaf pan. Bake 45 minutes or until bread feels firm.

Yield: 1 loaf

Zucchini Tea Bread

Floured baking spray
/4 cup chopped pecans
3½ cups all-purpose flour
1 teaspoon salt
1 teaspoon baking soda
/4 teaspoon baking powder
1 teaspoon ground cinnamon

2 eggs
¾ cup white sugar
¾ cup brown sugar
¼ cup oil
2 teaspoons vanilla extract
¾ cup sweetened applesauce
2½ cups zucchini, washed, ends removed, grated with skin on

- Preheat oven to 350°. Spray a 9- or 12-cup Bundt pan with floured baking spray and set aside.

- Spread pecans on a shallow baking pan and bake 6 to 8 minutes or until toasted. Remove from oven and place on a cooling rack to cool.

- In a large bowl, sift together flour, salt, baking soda, baking powder and cinnamon.

- In a large bowl, beat together eggs, white sugar, brown sugar, canola oil, vanilla and applesauce. Beat flour mixture into applesauce mixture in two additions, beating after each addition. Fold in toasted pecans and zucchini.

- Pour into prepared pan. Bake 60 to 70 minutes, or until a wooden pick inserted comes out clean.

- Remove from oven and place on a cooling rack for 15 minutes. Invert onto cooling rack, remove pan and cool.

Makes 20 slices

Best-Ever Yeast Rolls

2	packages active dry yeast		½	cup shortening
⅔	cup sugar, divided		1	cup boiling water
1	cup warm water (105° to 115°)		2	eggs, beaten
1	teaspoon salt		6-7	cups all-purpose flour, divided
½	cup butter or margarine, softened			

- Dissolve yeast and 1 teaspoon sugar in 1 cup warm water; let stand about 5 minutes.

- Combine remaining sugar, salt, butter and shortening in a large bowl. Add boiling water, stirring until butter and shortening melt. Cool slightly. Add dissolved yeast, stirring well.

- Add eggs and 3 cups flour, beating at medium speed of an electric mixer, until smooth. Gradually stir in enough remaining flour to make a soft dough. Place in a well-greased bowl, turning to grease top. Cover and let rise in a warm place (85°), free from drafts, 1 to 1½ hours or until doubled in bulk.

- Punch dough down; turn dough out onto a well-floured surface, and knead several times. Shape into 2-inch balls, and place in 3 greased 9-inch round baking pans. Cover and let rise in a warm place (85°), free from drafts, 30 to 40 minutes or until doubled in bulk.

- Bake at 325° 20 to 25 minutes or until golden.

Makes 3 dozen rolls

Homemade Loaf Bread

1 tablespoon shortening or margarine
⅓ cup sugar
1 cup water
1 package active dry yeast

1 egg
1 teaspoon salt
3 cups all-purpose flour

- Blend shortening and sugar together. Add ½ cup boiling water. Cool.

- Dissolve yeast in ½ cup lukewarm water. Add salt, egg and yeast to shortening and sugar. Sift flour and mix thoroughly. Beat while adding flour. Dough will be almost runny. Cover dough with thin cloth and refrigerate overnight.

- Next day, place dough on floured surface and knead well. Use a good deal of flour to take up slack. Grease an 8½ x 4¼ x 3-inch loaf pan with unsalted shortening. Place dough in pan and let rise to top of pan. Bake at 350° for 30 minutes.

Makes 1 loaf

Incredible Pimiento Cheese

8 ounces mild Cheddar cheese

8 ounces sharp Cheddar cheese

8 ounces processed cheese loaf

1½ tablespoons sugar

¼ teaspoon salt

¼ teaspoon black pepper

1 (4-ounce) jar diced pimiento, drained

1 cup mayonnaise

- Shred Cheddar cheeses in food processor. Cut cheese loaf into cubes. Position knife blade in food processor; gradually add cheese cubes to shredded cheeses. Add sugar, salt and pepper.

- Transfer to a mixing bowl. Stir in mayonnaise and pimiento.

Makes 1 quart

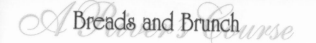

Scallion Muffins with Goat Cheese

1	cup milk, divided	½	teaspoon salt
4	ounces goat cheese	6	tablespoons unsalted butter
1½	cups all-purpose flour	1	egg
1	tablespoon baking powder	1	bunch scallions
1½	teaspoons sugar		

- Preheat oven to 400°. Grease muffin tins.
- Stir together 2 tablespoons milk and goat cheese.
- In a separate bowl, sift flour, baking powder, sugar and salt together. Melt butter and whisk with remaining milk and egg. Finely chop scallions to equal 1 cup. Stir butter mixture and scallions into flour.
- Divide batter in half. Pour a small amount into each muffin cup using one half of batter. Spoon 2 teaspoons cheese mixture into each cup on top of scallion batter. Use second half of batter to cover cheese mixture in each muffin cup.
- Bake 20 minutes.

Makes 12 muffins

Toasted Pecan Waffles

¾	cup all-purpose flour	3	cups chopped pecans, toasted
1	tablespoon baking powder	4	cups buttermilk
½	teaspoon baking soda	¾	cup butter or margarine, melted
1	teaspoon salt	4	large eggs, separated
3	tablespoons sugar		

- In a large mixing bowl, combine flour, baking powder, baking soda, salt and sugar. Stir well. Stir in chopped nuts.
- Combine buttermilk, melted butter and egg yolks; stir well. Add to flour mixture, stirring just until dry ingredients are moistened.
- Beat egg whites until stiff; fold into batter. Pour 1 cup batter into preheated, oiled waffle iron. Cook about 5 minutes or until golden. Repeat with remaining batter.

Makes 36 (4-inch) waffles

Crème Brûlée French Toast

1	stick unsalted butter		1	teaspoon vanilla extract
1	cup firmly packed brown sugar		1	teaspoon Grand Marnier or Amaretto
2	tablespoons corn syrup		¼	teaspoon salt
1	French baguette (at least 9-inches)			Ground cinnamon for garnishing
5	large eggs			Confectioners' sugar for garnishing
1½	cups half & half			

- In a small saucepan, melt butter; add brown sugar and corn syrup over moderate heat, stirring until smooth. Pour into a 13 x 9 x 2-inch baking dish. Slice bread ¾-inch thick on the diagonal from center portion of bread. Try to keep size uniform. Arrange bread slices in one layer in baking dish, squeezing them slightly to fit.

- Whisk together eggs, half & half, vanilla, Grand Marnier and salt until combined well and pour evenly over bread slices. Chill bread mixture, covered at least 8 hours or up to 1 day.

- Remove casserole from refrigerator at least 30 minutes before baking.

- Preheat oven to 350°. Bake, uncovered, until puffed and edges are pale golden, 35 to 40 minutes. Sprinkle with cinnamon and confectioners' sugar before serving. Serve hot French toast immediately.

Serves 6 to 8

Note: If watching cholesterol, you may use fat-free half & half and egg substitutes.

Sicilian Vegetable Pizza Roll

Filling

¼	cup olive oil
8	cups broccoli florets
1	cup peeled, sliced Jerusalem artichokes

5	large cloves garlic, minced
	Salt and pepper

- Make filling: In a large skillet, heat oil over medium heat. Add broccoli and sauté, stirring constantly, for 3 minutes or just until it begins to change color.

- Add Jerusalem artichokes and garlic; sprinkle with salt. Cover and cook, stirring often, for about 3 minutes or until crisp-tender. Sprinkle with pepper and cool completely.

Dough

3¼	cups unbleached all-purpose flour
2	teaspoons instant yeast
2	teaspoons sugar
1½	teaspoons salt

1⅓	cups water, room temperature (70° to 90°)
¼	cup whole wheat flour (or unbleached all-purpose flour), divided, for rolling dough
3	tablespoons olive oil, divided

- In a medium bowl, whisk together flour, yeast and sugar; then whisk in salt. Make a well in center of flour, add water and stir until blended.

- Sprinkle counter with some of the whole wheat (or all-purpose) flour. Scrape dough out onto counter and knead for 10 minutes until smooth and resilient. It will be very sticky during first 5 minutes of kneading. Add more flour if necessary only after first 5 minutes.

- Clean counter and sprinkle more flour on it. Set dough on top and allow to sit, covered with plastic wrap, 20 to 30 minutes.

- Preheat oven to 475°. Place oven rack at lowest level and place a baking stone on it before preheating.

- Using 1 tablespoon of olive oil, brush a 4-inch band of oil down center of a 20-inch long piece of heavy duty aluminum foil. Roll dough into an 18 x 16-inch rectangle. Arrange filling evenly over dough. Roll up dough from longer side. Pinch edge of dough firmly to make a tight seam. Turn dough seam side down. Pinch ends of dough firmly together and tuck them underneath.

- Roll loaf onto foil, seam side down, and lift it onto a baking sheet, leaving it on foil. Brush top with 1 tablespoon olive oil and make 3 small slashes in top of dough.

Sicilian Vegetable Pizza Roll continued

- Set baking sheet on hot stone or oven rack and bake 10 minutes. Reduce oven temperature to 400° and bake 10 minutes. Rotate pan and continue baking an additional 10 minutes or until loaf is golden all over.

- Remove from oven and brush top of loaf with remaining 1 tablespoon olive oil. Allow to cool about 10 minutes.

Variations: Use whatever vegetables you want for filling (spinach, onion, zucchini, mushrooms, etc.). Also, you can sprinkle with mozzarella cheese before rolling dough up. This bread is especially good dipped in marinara.

Make-Ahead Cheese Blintzes

2	(1¼-pound) loaves soft sandwich bread	½	cup sugar
2	(8-ounce) packages cream cheese, softened	1	teaspoon lemon juice
2	egg yolks	2	cups light brown sugar
		2	teaspoons ground cinnamon
		¼	cup butter, melted

- Trim crusts from bread; flatten with rolling pin. Mix cream cheese, egg yolks, sugar and lemon juice. Spread 1 teaspoon cheese mixture onto each piece of flattened bread.

- Mix brown sugar and cinnamon. Roll up bread slices; dip each piece into butter, then roll in cinnamon-sugar mixture. Cut each roll in half; freeze at least 3 hours on cookie sheet. Store in plastic bags until ready to use.

- When ready to use, remove from freezer; bake at 350° for 10 to 15 minutes.

Makes 80 to 100 rolls

Note: Great for last-minute treats.

Caramel Apple Breakfast Pudding

2	large tart apples	¼	cup pecan pieces
¼	cup water	3	eggs, beaten
¾	teaspoon ground cinnamon	1¼	cups milk
½	cup firmly packed brown sugar	1	teaspoon vanilla extract
2	tablespoons corn syrup	¼	teaspoon ground nutmeg
2	tablespoons butter	8-10	slices good Italian or French bread

- Peel, core and slice apples (about 2 cups). In a saucepan, combine apples and water; bring to a boil. Reduce heat and cook 5 to 7 minutes over low heat. Drain. Transfer apples to a small bowl and stir in cinnamon. Set aside.

- In same saucepan, combine brown sugar, corn syrup and butter. Cook, stirring, over medium heat until boiling. Remove from heat. Pour mixture into a 2-quart square baking dish. Sprinkle pecans over all.

- In a mixing bowl, combine eggs, milk, vanilla and nutmeg. Arrange a layer of half the bread slices on top of caramel mixture, trimming bread to fit. Spoon cooked apples evenly over bread layer. Arrange remaining bread slices on top.

- Pour egg mixture over bread, pressing down gently to moisten slices completely. Cover with plastic wrap and refrigerate 3 to 24 hours. Bake, uncovered, in a 325° oven 40 to 45 minutes. Let stand 15 minutes before serving.

Serves 8

Soups, Salads and Sandwiches

Midnight Hole in the
Great Smoky Mountains

Tucked in the crevices and valleys of the towering
Great Smoky Mountains are a vast array of springs. Just as in the
days of Ponce de Leon's fabled search for the Fountain of Youth,
visitors to the Carolinas have searched for medicinal healing
springs. For nearly two centuries travelers have enjoyed the
"waters" of the Carolinas. So renown were these waters that hotels
were built beginning in the late 1860s to accommodate the guests.
It was rumored that drinking and bathing in these waters held the
cure for rheumatism, nervousness, and indigestion. Today millions of
visitors still flock to these mountain streams and springs. Now they
come to linger by these cooling waters and refresh themselves on
hot summer days. Just as these visitors meander through the
mountains and streams of the Carolinas, come wander through the
following pages. Find a delectable recipe to pack in your picnic
basket on your next trip to the mountains.

Butternut Squash Soup

3 butternut squash, roasted	1 pint heavy cream
2-3 tablespoons butter	Salt and pepper to taste
1 large onion, cut julienne	
3 quarts vegetable stock or chicken stock	

- Preheat oven to 350°.
- Cut butternut squash in half. Roast in oven for 35 to 40 minutes. Remove seeds and peel.
- Add butter and onion to pot to sweat onion but not brown. Add squash and sweat. Pour in vegetable or chicken stock and add a small amount of salt and pepper. (Soup should be on the sweet side.)
- Stir in cream and cook for a while. Put through a food processor or food mill.

Makes 10 to 12 cups

Eggplant Soup

1 medium yellow onion, chopped	½ teaspoon salt
1 medium eggplant, chopped	Freshly ground black pepper
3 tablespoons olive oil	¼ teaspoon nutmeg
3-4 cups vegetable or chicken broth	Parmesan cheese (optional)
2 tablespoons tomato paste	Fresh nutmeg (optional)

- Sauté onion and eggplant in oil until soft. Add broth. Stir in tomato paste, salt and pepper.
- Cook 30 minutes over medium heat. Stir in nutmeg. Blend until smooth.
- Serve with Parmesan cheese and fresh nutmeg.

Serves 4

Vegetable Stock

Celery

Onions

Carrots

Parsley

Thyme

3 quarts water

- Place celery, onion, carrot, parsley and thyme in a medium saucepan. Add 3 quarts water, bring to a boil. Reduce heat to low and simmer 30 minutes. Strain the stock through a sieve or colander and discard vegetables.

Makes about 10 cups

Wonderful as a first course. Low in fat; high in fiber.

Broccoli Cream Cheese Soup

½ cup chopped green onions	1 teaspoon lemon juice
2 tablespoons butter	1 teaspoon salt
2 (8-ounce) packages cream cheese, cubed	½ teaspoon black pepper
2 cups half & half	4 chicken breasts, cooked, boned and cubed (optional)
2 cups chicken broth	Toasted almonds for garnish
3 (10-ounce) packages frozen chopped broccoli	Parsley for garnish

- Sauté onion in butter in large saucepan. Add cream cheese, half & half and broth.
- In separate saucepan, cook broccoli according to package directions and drain. Add broccoli, lemon juice, salt and pepper to broth mixture.
- You may add chicken at this time, if desired, and heat thoroughly. Garnish with almonds and parsley.

Serves 10

Gazpacho

2 cups finely chopped tomato	¾ cup water
1 cup finely chopped celery	¼ cup vinegar
1 cup finely chopped bell pepper	¼ cup vegetable oil
1 cup finely chopped cucumber	1 tablespoon salt
½ cup sliced green onion	2 teaspoons Worcestershire sauce
1 (4½-ounce) can chopped green chiles	Dash black pepper
3 (8-ounce) cans tomato sauce	

- Place ¾ of each chopped vegetable: tomato, celery, bell pepper, cucumber and onion into a food processor. Process until finely minced and pour into a separate bowl. Add remaining chopped vegetables to bowl.
- Stir in tomato sauce, water, vinegar, oil, salt, Worcestershire and pepper. Chill at least 2 hours.

Makes 10 cups

Cream of Asparagus Soup

½ pounds fresh asparagus
½ cups chicken stock
   cup chopped onions
-2 cups diced potatoes
½-1 cup sliced carrots

½ cup butter, divided
¼ cup flour
½ teaspoon salt
¼ teaspoon black pepper
1-2 cups half & half

Cut asparagus into pieces; pour in water just to cover; cook until tender. Place in blender with ½ cup chicken stock and purée. Pour into large saucepan.

Sauté onion, potato and carrot in ¼ cup butter until tender. Place into blender with ½ to 1 cup remaining chicken stock and purée, depending upon consistency desired. Combine with asparagus mixture.

Cook ¼ cup butter with flour, salt and pepper to make a roux. Add to saucepan in small amounts, blending well between each addition. Cook until desired consistency is achieved. May not need all of roux.

Add half & half. Heat thoroughly but do not boil.

Makes about 8 cups

Tortellini and Spinach Soup

1 (10-ounce) bag fresh spinach, washed
1 tablespoon olive oil
2 slices bacon, finely diced (optional)
1 teaspoon minced garlic
1 medium onion, diced
9 cups chicken broth
1 (28-ounce) can diced tomatoes

2 teaspoons dry Italian seasoning
1 (9-ounce) package premium refrigerated spinach or cheese tortellini
1 (15½-ounce) can great Northern beans, not drained
Salt and pepper to taste
Freshly grated Parmesan cheese

- Wash spinach thoroughly, remove stems and coarsely chop.

- Heat oil in stockpot over medium-high heat. Add bacon, if desired, cooking until lightly brown. Add garlic and onion and cook until brown, 10 to 15 minutes.

- Stir in broth, tomatoes and seasoning; bring to a boil. Add tortellini and simmer just until tender, 7 to 10 minutes.

- Add spinach, salt and pepper to taste, and beans. Spinach will wilt and cook immediately. Top with Parmesan cheese and serve.

Serves 6 to 8

Vichyssoise

4 medium leeks, white part only
1 medium onion, quartered
½ stick butter
4 Idaho potatoes
2 (14½-ounce) cans chicken broth

1 teaspoon chopped chives
2 cups half & half
Salt to taste
Freshly ground white pepper to taste

- Slice leeks and onion. Sauté in butter in a large soup pot until tender. Pare, slice and chop potatoes; add to onion mixture. Stir in broth. Cook until potatoes are tender.

- Cool slightly and purée in food processor. Add chives and half & half. Season with salt and white pepper.

- Good served hot or cold.

Serves 8

Murrells Inlet Clam Chowder

	slices bacon	1	teaspoon salt
	medium potatoes, diced	1	teaspoon black pepper
	medium onions, diced	1	teaspoon brown sugar
	(28-ounce) can tomatoes	½	teaspoon vinegar (optional)
	(8-ounce) bottle clam juice	¼	teaspoon hot sauce
½	cup catsup	2	whole celery stalks
½	tablespoons Worcestershire sauce	3	cups water
½	tablespoons steak sauce	3	(6½-ounce) cans minced clams, undrained

In a large pot, fry bacon, drain on paper towel and crumble. Add potatoes and onion to bacon drippings. Cook over medium heat 10 minutes or until soft.

In blender, combine tomatoes, clam juice, catsup, Worcestershire, steak sauce, salt, pepper, bacon, brown sugar, vinegar and hot sauce. Process 50 seconds or until well blended. Add to potato and onion in pot. Add celery and water to pot.

Simmer, stirring frequently, over low heat 45 minutes to 1 hour. Add clams, continue simmering 1 to 2 more hours, stirring frequently.

Remove celery and discard. Adjust seasonings to taste.

Serves 8

Mushroom Bisque

1 pound fresh mushrooms	2 tablespoons sherry
8 tablespoons butter, divided	1½ teaspoons salt
2 shallots, minced	10 drops hot pepper sauce
4 cups chicken broth	Ground white pepper to taste
6 tablespoons all-purpose flour	1 (6-ounce) box long-grain and wild rice mix, cooked (optional)
3 cups milk	Chopped parsley for garnish
1 cup heavy cream	

- Wipe mushrooms with a damp towel; trim and slice. In skillet, melt 2 tablespoons butter. Add mushrooms and shallots. Sauté 5 minutes. Place mushrooms, shallots and broth into a blender and blend until smooth.

- Melt remaining butter in a saucepan and stir in flour.

- In a separate saucepan, bring milk to a boil. Add hot milk, all at once, to the butter-flour mixture, whisking vigorously until smooth.

- Add heavy cream, mushroom mixture, sherry, salt and hot pepper sauce. Season with pepper.

- If desired, add cooked rice. Garnish with parsley.

Makes about 2½ quarts

Note: This soup takes a little extra work, but the results are worth it!

Good Old-Fashioned Potato Soup

Soup

1	large onion, diced	1	(10-ounce) package frozen corn
2-3	stalks celery, diced		Milk
3	tablespoons oil	1	tablespoon butter
15	medium potatoes, peeled and diced		
	Salt and pepper to taste		

- Sauté onion and celery in oil about 5 minutes. Add potatoes and cover with water. Cook 15 minutes. Add frozen corn.
- Thin mixture with milk and add some butter until desired consistency is achieved.

Revels

2	cups flour	3	eggs
1	teaspoon salt		

- Combine flour, salt and eggs; add some water or milk until a dough forms. This makes revels (homemade noodles).
- Drop revels in small bite-sized pieces into soup mixture. Cook, stirring, 10 to 15 minutes.

Serves 12

Great down-home recipe. Kids love the revels or homemade noodles.

Baked Potato Soup

Oven-Fried Bacon

- Preheat oven to 400° and place rack in middle level.

- Place strips of bacon in a jelly-roll pan with sides about ¾ inches high. Roast until fat begins to render, about 5 to 6 minutes.

- Rotate pan front to back; continue roasting until crisp, 5 to 6 minutes longer for thin-sliced bacon, or 8 to 10 minutes for thick sliced. Thick sliced pancetta and bacon may require at least 20 minutes total cooking time.

- Transfer with tongs to a paper towel to drain.

4	baking potatoes, baked	1½	cups shredded Cheddar cheese, divided
⅔	cup butter	12	slices bacon, cooked, crumbled, and divided
⅔	cup flour		
6	cups milk	4-6	green onions, sliced
1	cup sour cream		Salt and pepper to taste

- Remove pulp from potato skins and set aside.

- Melt butter over medium heat; add flour and stir, over low heat, for 1 to 2 minutes. Gradually add milk and simmer until thickened. Add potato pulp (it will appear lumpy).

- Add sour cream, 1 cup cheese, half the bacon and half the onion. Stir until cheese melts. Season with salt and pepper to taste.

- Soup will be thick. If you want to thin it, add more milk. Garnish with remaining cheese, onion and bacon.

Note: Save the potato skins and fill them with cheese, onion and bacon. Bake in a preheated oven at 425° about 10 minutes or until hot and cheese is melted.

Chicken with Leek Soup In A Hurry

¼	cup butter	2	carrots, diced
¼	cup all-purpose flour	1	leek, diced
2	quarts canned chicken broth	2	stalks celery, diced
½	teaspoon dried thyme	½	cup potatoes, peeled, diced
1	bay leaf	¼	cup chopped onion
2	cloves garlic, minced		Cooked chicken, cut into bite-sized pieces

- In a large soup pot, melt butter over medium heat. Add flour and stir constantly to make a light brown roux.
- Gradually add broth and whisk to blend well. Add thyme and bay leaf and simmer 30 minutes. Add garlic, carrot, leek, celery, potato and onion to soup and simmer until tender but not overcooked, about 20 minutes.
- Season with salt and pepper. Add chicken meat and continue simmering until chicken is heated through. Remove bay leaf before serving.

Serves 6

Eden Street Egg Drop Soup

5	cups chicken stock	1	teaspoon salt
3	tablespoons cornstarch	¼	teaspoon white pepper
3	tablespoons cold water	3	eggs, beaten
½	teaspoon sugar	4	green onions, diced with tops

- Bring stock to a boil in a large Dutch oven or soup pot.
- Place cornstarch in a small bowl and slowly add cold water, mixing until smooth; add sugar, salt and pepper. Gradually add into stock until smoothly blended.
- Return to a boil then immediately reduce heat. Add eggs; stir just a minute until eggs separate.
- Serve sprinkled with green onions.

Serves 6

Chicken and Wild Rice Soup

½   cup chopped celery

½   cup chopped onion

½   cup chopped carrot

¼   cup chopped bell pepper

2   quarts chicken broth

1   (6-ounce) box long-grain and wild rice mix (do not use seasoning pack)

½   cup butter

½   cup flour

1   quart whole milk

4   cups cooked chicken, cut into pieces

12   ounces fresh mushrooms, sautéed in butter

- Add celery, onion, carrot and bell pepper to a Dutch oven with broth and rice. Simmer 30 to 40 minutes.
- While rice cooks, make a white sauce by melting butter in pan; whisk in flour; slowly add milk. Stir until thickened, about 8 to 10 minutes.
- Add white sauce, chicken and mushrooms to soup and heat through. Freezes well.

Makes 3 quarts

French Onion Soup

4 tablespoons butter

5-6 medium onions, thinly sliced

3 cloves garlic, crushed

1 teaspoon salt

½ teaspoon sugar

1 sprig fresh thyme (optional)

2 tablespoons flour

2 cups canned low-sodium beef broth

6 cups low-sodium canned chicken broth

½ cup dry white wine (or red)

Salt and pepper to taste

1 baguette, cut diagonally into ¾-inch slices

1½ cups Gruyère cheese, grated (Swiss cheese may be substituted)

½ cup Asiago cheese, grated (Parmesan cheese may be substituted)

Red onions taste the best, but make the color murky. If using red onions, add 1 tablespoon balsamic vinegar when adjusting flavor with salt and pepper.

- Melt butter in large Dutch oven over medium-high heat; add onion, garlic, salt and sugar, stirring to thoroughly coat onions with butter. Cook, stirring frequently, until onions are tender and syrupy and inside of pot is coated with very deep brown crust, 30 to 35 minutes.

- Stir in broths, wine and thyme (if desired), scraping pot bottom with wooden spoon to loosen brown bits and bring to simmer. Simmer 20 minutes, and discard thyme. Adjust seasonings with salt and pepper. Mixture may be cooled to room temperature and refrigerated in airtight container up to 2 days; return to simmer before finishing soup with bread and cheese.

- To serve, adjust oven rack to upper middle position. Set serving bowls on baking sheet and fill oven-proof bowls with about 1½ cups soup. Top each bowl with 1 or 2 slices of untoasted French bread (in a single layer) and cover with Gruyère and Parmesan cheeses.

- Broil until well browned and bubbly, about 10 minutes. Cool 5 minutes and serve.

Serves 8

Tortilla Soup

---

1   onion, chopped
1   bell pepper, chopped
2   teaspoons oil
2   (10-ounce) cans diced tomatoes with green chiles
2   (15-ounce) cans black beans, rinsed and drained
1   (16-ounce) can pinto beans, rinsed and drained
2   (1¼ to 1½-ounce) packages taco seasoning mix
2   (1-ounce) envelopes Ranch-style dressing mix

2   (15¼-ounce) cans whole kernel corn, drained
5   cups water
    Salt and pepper to taste
2   pounds chicken breast, cooked and shredded
    Sour cream (optional)
    Tortilla chips
    Monterey Jack cheese

- In a large Dutch oven or soup pot, sauté onion and bell pepper in oil until tender. Add tomatoes, beans, seasoning mixes, corn, water, salt and pepper and bring to a boil.

- Add chicken and simmer, covered, until completely heated through.

- Serve with sour cream, tortilla chips and Monterey Jack cheese.

Serves 15 to 20

Refried Bean Soup

2	teaspoons olive oil	1	(14½-ounce) Mexican-style stewed tomatoes
1	large onion, chopped	1	(15-ounce) can black beans, rinsed and drained
1	medium bell pepper, chopped	1	(16-ounce) can red kidney beans, rinsed and drained
2	teaspoons minced garlic	1	(16-ounce) can fat-free refried beans
1	(14½-ounce) can vegetable broth or fat-free chicken broth	¼	teaspoon ground cumin
			Black pepper to taste

- Heat oil in a 4½-quart Dutch oven or soup pot over medium heat. Add onion and bell pepper; raise heat to medium-high and cook 2 to 3 minutes until tender.

- Add garlic, broth and tomatoes and stir. Raise heat to high and add beans to pot. Stir in refried beans and cumin. Add black pepper to taste. Stir well.

- Cover and bring to a boil. Reduce heat to low and stir occasionally 5 to 7 minutes or until ready to serve.

Serves 4

Fruit Soup

2	tablespoons quick-cooking tapioca	½	cup frozen orange juice concentrate
1½	cups water	2½	cups diced fresh fruit of choice (peaches, cherries, bananas, apples, melon balls) or frozen fruit
1	tablespoon sugar		
	Dash salt		

- Mix tapioca and water in saucepan and let stand 5 minutes. Bring to a boil, stirring constantly. Remove from heat.

- Add sugar, salt and orange juice; mix until well blended. Cool, stirring once after 15 to 20 minutes. Cover and chill.

- Before serving, add fruits. If thinner soup is desired, add more juice or less fruit.

Serves 5 to 6

Note: For prettiest results, choose small, colorful fruits. Berries and melon balls are good.

Fireside Split Pea Soup

1	pound bag dried split peas	6	carrots, peeled and diced
8	cups defatted chicken broth (or water or half water/half broth, depending on ham bone)	3	onions, coarsely chopped
		2	leeks (3 inches of green left on) well washed and cut into ½-inch dice
1	meaty ham bone or large ham hock	3	cloves garlic, peeled and minced
2	ribs celery, chopped	3	medium zucchini, cut into ½-inch dice
1	bay leaf	1	(10-ounce) bag fresh spinach, stems removed, cut into 1-inch strips, or 1 (10-ounce) package frozen chopped spinach
½	cup chopped flat-leaf parsley, divided		
1	teaspoon dried tarragon		
1	teaspoon dried thyme	4	ripe tomatoes, seeded and diced or 1 (28-ounce) can diced tomatoes with juice
2	tablespoons olive oil		
1	tablespoon butter		Salt and pepper to taste

- Pick through split peas and discard any pebbles. Rinse through a strainer.

- Combine peas and broth in a large heavy soup pot and bring to a boil. Add ham bone, celery, bay leaf, ¼ cup parsley, tarragon and thyme. Reduce heat to medium-low and simmer 45 minutes, partially covered, stirring occasionally.

- Meanwhile, heat oil and butter in a separate pot over medium-low heat. Add carrots, onion, leeks and garlic. Cook, partially covered, until vegetables are tender, stirring occasionally. Season with salt and pepper. Add to soup and simmer, partially covered, about 30 minutes, stirring once or twice. Remove ham bone and set aside.

- Add zucchini and cook 15 minutes, stirring from the bottom.

- Add spinach and simmer 10 minutes. Add tomatoes and remaining parsley. Season with salt and pepper. When ham bone has cooled enough to handle, shred meat from bone and stir into soup. Heat through and serve.

Serves 10

Vegetarian Chili

1 large onion, chopped
3 cloves garlic, minced
2 tablespoons olive oil
1 large bell pepper, chopped
½ cup grated carrot
1 (15-ounce) can black beans, undrained
1 (16-ounce) can pinto beans, undrained
1 (16-ounce) can kidney beans, undrained
1 (14½-ounce) can diced tomatoes

1 (10-ounce) can diced tomatoes with green chiles
½ cup sliced jalapeños, or to taste
3 tablespoons chili powder
1 tablespoon cayenne pepper, or to taste
 hot sauce to taste
3 cups water
½ teaspoon cumin
 Shredded cheese (optional)
 Sour cream (optional)

- Sauté onion and garlic in oil in large stock pot until soft; add bell pepper and cook 2 minutes.

- Add carrot, black beans, pinto beans, kidney beans, tomatoes, jalapeños, chili powder, cayenne pepper, hot sauce, 2 cups water, and cumin.

- Simmer 2 hours; adding remaining water as needed. Serve with cheese and/or sour cream.

Serves 6

Mexican Chicken Chili

1 pound chicken breasts
1 tablespoon olive oil
10 cups water
2 cups chicken stock
½ cup tomato sauce
1 potato, peeled and chopped
1 small onion, diced
1 cup frozen yellow corn
1 carrot, sliced
1 celery stalk, diced
1 cup canned diced tomatoes

1 (16-ounce) can red kidney beans, undrained
1 (4-ounce) jar diced pimientos
1 jalapeño, diced
¼ cup chopped parsley
1 clove garlic, minced
1½ teaspoons chili powder
1 teaspoon cumin
¼ teaspoon salt
Dash basil
Dash oregano
Dash cayenne pepper

- In a large soup pot, sauté chicken in oil until cooked. Remove chicken and cool; shred meat.

- Do not rinse soup pot; use some water to deglaze pot. Return meat to pot with remaining liquid and add all ingredients.

- Bring to a boil; reduce heat and simmer 4 to 5 hours. Stir often. Chili should reduce and thicken.

Serves 6

Mixed Greens and Strawberries with Balsamic Vinaigrette

¼	cup balsamic vinegar		1½	cups sliced celery
½	teaspoon salt		⅓	cup pine nuts, lightly toasted
½	teaspoon ground black pepper		½	cup coarsely grated Parmesan cheese
¾	cup extra-virgin olive oil		1½	cups halved strawberries
10	cups mixed salad greens, torn into small pieces			

- Whisk together vinegar, salt and pepper. Add oil in a thin stream, whisking until emulsified.
- Just before serving, combine greens, celery, pine nuts, cheese and strawberries. Toss dressing with salad, using just enough to coat but not wilt greens.
- Serve on a clear glass plate.

Serves 10 to 12 people

Crunchy Romaine Salad

1	cup walnuts		1	(1-pound) bag Romaine or Leafy Lettuce (or mixed)
1	(3-ounce) package chicken ramen noodle soup mix, uncooked, crushed		4	green onions, chopped
4	tablespoons butter, melted		1	bunch broccoli, washed and cut into florets

- Brown walnuts and noodles in butter.
- Mix lettuce, onion and broccoli in a large bowl and toss well. Pour dressing over salad and top with noodles and nuts.

Salad Dressing

1	cup oil		3	teaspoons soy sauce
1	cup sugar			Salt
½	cup red or white wine vinegar			Freshly ground black pepper

- Whisk together oil, sugar, vinegar, soy sauce, salt and pepper until well blended.

Serves 6 to 8

Mandarin Mixed Greens with Vinaigrette

Vinaigrette

⅔ cup olive oil

⅓ cup cider vinegar

⅓ cup sugar

1 teaspoon parsley

1 teaspoon salt

¼ teaspoon black pepper

¼ teaspoon crushed red pepper

• Combine oil, vinegar, sugar, parsley, salt, black pepper and red pepper and mix thoroughly.

Salad

⅔ cup sliced almonds

⅓ cup sugar

8 cups fresh salad greens

8 ounces fresh mushrooms, sliced

1 (15-ounce) can Mandarin oranges, drained

• Cook almonds in sugar in nonstick skillet 5 to 7 minutes until browned. Spoon on to waxed paper and cool.

• Toss greens, mushrooms and oranges. Break apart sugared almonds and add to salad. When ready to serve, toss with vinaigrette.

Serves 8

Cantaloupe Cooler Salad

1 large or 2 small cantaloupes, sliced
Lettuce leaves, torn into bite size pieces

1 large onion (Vidalia if available), thinly sliced and
separated into rings
12 slices bacon, cooked and crumbled

- Combine cantaloupe slices, lettuce, onion rings and bacon in a large bowl. Toss with Poppy Seed Dressing.

Poppy Seed Dressing

¾ cup vegetable oil
⅓ cup honey
¼ cup red wine vinegar
2 tablespoons poppy seeds

1 tablespoon minced or grated onion
1 tablespoon Dijon mustard
1 teaspoon salt

- Combine oil, honey, vinegar, poppy seeds, onion, mustard and salt. Whisk together to blend well.

Serves 6

Avocado, Tomato and Red Onion Salad

2 ripe avocados
2 ripe tomatoes
1 small red onion
1½ tablespoons red wine vinegar

2 tablespoons virgin olive oil
Salt and freshly ground black pepper to taste
Dash hot sauce
Boston lettuce leaves for serving (optional)

- Cut flesh of avocados and tomatoes into cubes and put into a mixing bowl. Peel onion, cut in half lengthwise, then slice each half crosswise into very thin half moons. Toss to separate slices and add to mixing bowl.
- Drizzle vinegar and oil over salad. Season with salt, pepper and four or more dashes of hot sauce. Gently mix vegetables to distribute seasoning. Taste and adjust seasoning as desired.
- Spoon salad into whole, cup-shaped leaves of Boston lettuce, if desired.

Serves 4 to 6

Zucchini, Tomato and Corn Salad

1½ pounds medium zucchini
1½ teaspoons salt, divided
1 cup fresh corn kernels (cut from 2 ears)
2 tablespoons fresh lemon juice
½ teaspoon salt

¼ teaspoon black pepper
¼ cup extra-virgin olive oil
8 ounces grape or cherry tomatoes, halved lengthwise (2 cups)
¼ cup thinly sliced fresh basil

- Working with 1 zucchini at a time, cut lengthwise into julienne strips with slicer, turning zucchini and avoiding core. Discard core. Toss zucchini strips with 1 teaspoon salt and let drain in a colander set over a bowl, covered and chilled, 1 hour.
- Gently squeeze handfuls of zucchini to remove excess water and pat dry with paper towels.
- Cook corn in a small saucepan of boiling water until tender, about 3 minutes. Drain and rinse under cold water. Pat dry.
- Whisk together lemon juice, sugar, pepper and remaining ½ teaspoon salt in a large bowl. Gradually add oil in a slow stream, constantly whisking. Add zucchini, corn, tomatoes and basil. Toss well.

Serves 4 to 6

Note: Salad (without dressing and basil) may be made 4 hours ahead and kept, covered, at room temperature.

Spinach Salad with Berries and Curry Dressing

6   ounces fresh spinach (about six cups), torn into bite-size pieces
1   cup thickly sliced strawberries

1   cup blueberries
1   small red onion, thinly sliced
½   cup chopped pecans

• Wash and dry spinach. Toss with Nonfat Curry Dressing. Add berries, onion and pecans. Toss lightly and serve.

Nonfat Curry Dressing

2   tablespoons balsamic vinegar
2   tablespoons rice vinegar
1   tablespoon plus 1 teaspoon honey

1   teaspoon curry powder
2   teaspoons Dijon mustard
    Salt and pepper to taste

• Whisk together vinegars, honey, curry powder, mustard, salt and pepper until well blended.

Serves 6 to 8

Spinach Salad

1-1½ pounds fresh spinach
3   hard-boiled eggs, grated

8   slices bacon, cooked and crumbled
    Croutons

- Layer spinach, eggs, bacon and croutons in a large salad bowl. Pour dressing over salad and toss lightly.

Dressing
1   cup vegetable oil
5   tablespoons red wine vinegar
4   tablespoons sour cream
1½ teaspoons salt
½   teaspoon dry mustard

½   teaspoon celery seed
2   tablespoons sugar
2   teaspoons parsley
2   cloves garlic, crushed
    Coarsely ground black pepper to taste

- Combine oil, vinegar, sour cream, salt, mustard, celery seed, sugar, parsley, garlic and pepper in a 1-quart jar and shake vigorously to mix well.
- Pour over spinach greens.

Serves 6

Marinated Broccoli

---

2   bunches fresh broccoli
1   cup cider vinegar
1   tablespoon sugar
1   tablespoon dill weed

1   teaspoon salt
1   teaspoon black pepper
1   teaspoon garlic salt
1½ cups vegetable oil

- Cut broccoli into small florets. Mix vinegar, sugar, dill, salt, pepper, garlic salt and oil until well blended. Pour over broccoli. Cover and refrigerate 24 hours. Drain and serve.

Variation: Other raw vegetables may be used with broccoli: carrot strips, cherry tomatoes, mushrooms, etc.

Serves 6

Marinated Asparagus

bunch asparagus, blanched

Dressing

¼ cup chopped walnuts
¼ cup soy sauce
2 tablespoons vegetable oil

¼ cup cider vinegar
¼ cup sugar
⅛ teaspoon black pepper

• Place blanched asparagus into oblong dish. Mix walnuts, soy sauce, oil, vinegar, sugar and pepper and pour over asparagus. Marinate 3 hours in refrigerator.

Serves 4

Asparagus Salad

2 (14½-ounce) cans asparagus, drained
1 bell pepper, chopped
1 small bunch green onions, chopped
1 stalk celery, chopped
¾ cup vegetable oil

½ cup red wine vinegar
½ cup sugar
½ clove garlic, minced
1 (2-ounce) jar sliced pimientos

• Place asparagus in a 13 x 9 x 2-inch baking dish. Combine bell pepper, onion, celery, oil, vinegar, sugar and garlic and mix well. Pour over asparagus.

• Chill 4 hours or overnight before serving.

• Garnish with pimiento slices.

Serves 6 to 8

Lime Buttermilk Salad

2 (6-ounce) packages lime-flavored gelatin
1 cup buttermilk
1 (8-ounce) can crushed pineapple, drained, reserving juice
2 cups hot water

1 cup finely chopped celery
1 cup sliced almonds
1 cup finely chopped bell pepper
   Mayonnaise

- Dissolve gelatin in 2 cups hot water. Add buttermilk and pineapple juice. Allow to stand for 30 minutes.
- Add celery, almonds, bell pepper and crushed pineapple.
- Place in molds or 9 x 13-inch casserole dish and refrigerate.
- Serve on lettuce with a teaspoon of mayonnaise.

Serves 12

Tailgate Slaw

1 large head cabbage, shredded
1 large onion, separated into rings
½ cup plus 1 teaspoon sugar, divided
1 cup white vinegar

¾ vegetable oil
1 tablespoon salt
1 teaspoon dry mustard
2 teaspoons celery seed

- Place cabbage and onion rings in a large bowl. Sprinkle ½ cup sugar on top.
- In a small saucepan, combine vinegar, oil, salt, mustard, celery seed and 1 teaspoon sugar. Bring to a boil and cook 3 minutes. Pour over cabbage and mix well. Cover and let stand overnight.
- Will keep for days in refrigerator.

Serves 10 to 12

Shrimp Salad

1	cup water	¾	cup finely chopped celery
1	cup vinegar		Salt and pepper to taste
3	tablespoons Old Bay seasoning	1	tablespoon fresh lemon juice
2	pounds shrimp	½-¾	cup mayonnaise
2	hard-boiled eggs, chopped	1	rounded tablespoon dill
1	shallot, finely chopped		

- In a large saucepan, bring water, vinegar and Old Bay seasoning to a boil. Add shrimp and stir. Cover and remove from heat. Let steam about 5 minutes. Cover with ice to cool.

- When cooled, drain, peel shrimp and place in a mixing bowl.

- In a separate bowl, add egg, shallot, celery, salt, pepper, lemon juice, mayonnaise and dill and mix well. Combine with shrimp and chill before serving.

- Serve with egg quarters, sliced cucumber and avocado.

Serves 8 to 10

Bunny Hop Rice Salad

2	(6-ounce) boxes long-grain and wild rice mix, with seasoning packet	½	cup golden raisins
		1	cup honey roasted peanuts
1	yellow bell pepper, chopped	½	cup oil
1	red bell pepper, chopped	½	cup honey
2	green onions, chopped	½	cup white wine vinegar
1	(16-ounce) package frozen green peas, thawed	2	teaspoons curry powder

- Cook rice according to package directions.

- Combine rice, bell peppers, onion, peas, raisins and peanuts (or add peanuts just before serving to remain crunchy).

- Combine oil, honey, vinegar and curry for dressing. Whisk until well blended and pour over salad.

Serves 10 to 14

Lentil Salad

1½ cups lentils, rinsed
3½ cups water
1 cup chopped onion
2 sprigs fresh thyme (optional)

1 bay leaf
½ teaspoon salt
Pinch ground cloves (optional)

- Place lentils, water, onion, thyme, bay leaf, salt and cloves, if desired, in a medium saucepan. Bring to a boil, cover, and simmer about 25 minutes or until lentils are cooked but still hold their shape. Cool to lukewarm and drain off liquid. Pour into a mixing bowl.

Dressing

2 tablespoons white wine vinegar, plus more to taste
4 tablespoons virgin olive oil, plus more to taste
Salt and freshly ground black pepper to taste
1 tablespoon Dijon mustard
Dashes hot sauce

1 large ripe tomato, chopped
⅓ cup finely chopped shallots, scallions or onion
3 cloves garlic, minced
2 tablespoons chopped fresh chives for garnish

- Whisk together vinegar, oil, salt, pepper, mustard and hot sauce. Stir in tomato, shallots and garlic.
- Pour dressing over warm lentils and fold in gently.
- Taste and adjust seasoning. Sprinkle with chopped chives before serving.

Serves 8 to 10

B.L.T. Salad

6	slices bacon	¼	cup mayonnaise
¼	loaf Italian bread	1	tablespoon water
	Kosher salt to taste	1	small red onion
¼	teaspoon minced garlic	½	pound cherry tomatoes (about ¾ pint)
1	tablespoon fresh lemon juice	1	head Boston lettuce

- In a skillet, cook bacon over moderate heat until crisp. Reserving 1 tablespoon drippings in skillet, drain bacon on paper towels and crumble.

- Cut bread into ¾-inch cubes to measure 1 cup. Heat drippings over moderately high heat but not smoking and sauté bread crumbs with salt to taste, until golden brown. Transfer croutons to paper towels to drain and cool.

- In a small bowl, whisk together garlic, lemon juice, mayonnaise, water, salt and pepper to taste. Slice onion and cut tomatoes in half. Tear lettuce into bite-sized pieces.

- In a large bowl, toss together onion, tomatoes, lettuce, half of bacon and half of croutons, salt and pepper to taste, and enough dressing to coat.

- Divide salad between two plates and top with remaining croutons and bacon.

Serves 2 as a main course

Mediterranean Pasta Salad

1 (16-ounce) package vermicelli
½-¾ cup olive oil
3 heaping tablespoons Greek seasoning
4 tablespoons lemon juice

¼ cup mayonnaise
1 (4-ounce) jar diced pimientos, drained
2 (3.8-ounce) cans sliced black olives, drained
6 green onions, sliced thin (white and green parts)

• Boil vermicelli for 6 minutes with no salt. Drain and rinse with cold water.

• Combine oil, Greek seasoning, lemon juice and mayonnaise with a wire whisk. Add pimientos, olives and onions. Pour over pasta and refrigerate several hours or overnight.

• Remove from refrigerator 30 minutes before serving and toss well.

Serves 10 to 12

Summer's Best Pasta Salad

1 (10-ounce) package rotini pasta
3 pounds tomatoes, seeded and chopped

4 slices bacon, cooked and crumbled
4 cups mixed salad greens

• Cook pasta, drain and rinse with cold water. Place in a large serving bowl. Add tomatoes, bacon and greens.

Dressing
⅔ cup mayonnaise
½ cup sour cream
2 tablespoons Dijon mustard
2 teaspoons sugar

1 tablespoon cider vinegar
½ teaspoon salt
½ teaspoon black pepper

• In a small bowl, combine mayonnaise, sour cream, mustard, sugar, vinegar, salt and pepper; mix well. Spoon over pasta and toss to coat.

Serves 6

Colorful Pasta Salad

1   (16-ounce) package tri-color rotini
    pastas
1   (15-ounce) can black beans or black-
    eyed peas, rinsed and drained

1   (8-ounce) package provolone cheese,
    diced
½   cup red onion, diced
    Red and green bell peppers, diced
    Parsley for garnish

• Cook pasta according to package directions until al dente. Cool.

• In a large bowl, combine beans, cheese, onion and bell peppers until well mixed. Stir in
  pasta, pour dressing over all and chill.

Dressing
½   cup vinegar
¼   cup vegetable oil
¼   cup sugar

¼   teaspoon black pepper
1   (0.7-ounce) envelope Italian salad
    dressing mix

• Whisk together vinegar, oil, sugar, pepper and dressing mix until well blended. Pour over
  pasta and toss; chill. Garnish with parsley, if desired.

Variation: Fresh broccoli florets may also be used.

Serves 10 to 12

Carrot Copper Pennies

2 pounds carrots,
peeled and sliced

Salt to taste

1 small bell pepper,
sliced into rings

1 medium onion,
thinly sliced

1 (10¾-ounce) can
tomato soup

½ cup salad oil

1 cup sugar

¾ cup vinegar

1 teaspoon prepared
mustard

1 teaspoon
Worcestershire sauce

Black pepper to taste

• Boil carrots in salted
water until tender and
cool. Place carrots in
dish with alternating
layers of bell pepper and
onion. Combine soup,
oil, sugar, vinegar,
mustard, Worcestershire
and pepper, adding
more salt if needed. Beat
until well blended and
pour over vegetables.
Refrigerate, covered,
up to one week.

Serves 12 to 15

Orzo Salad

Dressing

1   cup vegetable oil
½   cup red wine vinegar

2   teaspoons freshly ground black pepper
1   tablespoon salt

- Combine oil, vinegar, pepper and salt until well blended. Pour dressing over pasta while hot.

Salad

1   (1-pound) box orzo pasta, cooked and drained
⅓   cup chopped fresh parsley
⅓   cup chopped fresh dill
1   (14-ounce) can artichoke hearts, drained and chopped
1   (14-ounce) can hearts of palm, drained and chopped
1   (3½-ounce) jar capers, drained

2   cups chopped bell pepper
¾   cup chopped red onion
3   teaspoons minced garlic
½   teaspoon dried oregano
½   teaspoon dried basil

- Cook pasta according to package directions; drain. Pour dressing over pasta while hot.
- Combine parsley, dill, artichoke, hearts of palm, capers, bell pepper, onion, garlic, oregano and basil and mix well. Add to pasta and marinate several hours or overnight.

Serves a bunch!

Charity League Pasta Salad

cups fusilli pasta (corkscrew),
  uncooked

large or 2 small zucchini

small yellow summer squash

cup red onion, minced

cup celery, minced

1 (1-ounce) envelope Ranch-style
  dressing mix

1 cup sour cream

1 cup mayonnaise

1 teaspoon garlic salt

Cook pasta according to package directions. Drain.

Cut zucchini in half lengthwise, then again to make 4 long pieces. Slice very thin to resemble triangles. Cut yellow squash in same fashion. Place zucchini and yellow squash in a large bowl and add onion and celery. Add pasta and stir.

Mix dressing mix, sour cream, mayonnaise and garlic salt until well blended; add to pasta mixture. Refrigerate overnight.

Serves 10 to 12

Pasta salads ... whether carefully created from a long-time favorite recipe or tossed together in a pinch using on-hand ingredients ... make the perfect sides. These oh-so-versatile dishes have been woven into the tradition of the Junior Charity League of Shelby, finding their way onto our tea room menus through the years and as accompaniments to complete our often-served boxed lunch fare.

Dilly Seafood Pasta Salad

Dressing

1   lemon
½   cup mayonnaise

½   cup sour cream
1   tablespoon dill weed

• Zest whole lemon. Juice lemon to measure 1 tablespoon juice. Combine zest, juice, mayonnaise, sour cream and dill in a 1-quart bowl; mix well.

Salad

2   cups medium shell pasta, uncooked
1   cup cucumber
½   cup red bell pepper, chopped
½   cup carrot, coarsely chopped

¼   cup green onions with tops, thinly sliced
8   ounces cooked medium shrimp, shelled and deveined
¼   teaspoon salt

• Cook pasta according to package directions in 4-quart pot; drain and rinse with cold water. Score down length of cucumber in evenly spaced rows around entire cucumber. Slice cucumber.

• In a large bowl, combine pasta, cucumber, bell pepper, carrot, onion, shrimp and salt. Pour dressing over salad and toss gently using tongs. Cover and refrigerate at least 30 minutes or overnight.

Serves 6

Chicken and Pecan Salad

cups cubed chicken or turkey
cup diced celery
¼ cup pecan pieces
½ cup mayonnaise
tablespoons salad oil

1 tablespoon vinegar
½ teaspoon salt
Lettuce leaf
Fresh peaches for garnish

In a large serving bowl, combine chicken, celery and pecans.

In a small bowl, combine mayonnaise, oil, vinegar and salt. Pour over chicken mixture and toss lightly. Place on lettuce leaf. Garnish with fresh peaches or Kiwi Melon Salad

Serves 4

Kiwi Melon Salad

⅔ cup sugar
⅓ cup water
1 tablespoon lemon zest
¼ cup lemon juice
¼ cup rum
4 kiwis, peeled and sliced
4 cups melon balls: honeydew, watermelon, cantaloupe

• Combine sugar and water; bring to a boil. Simmer 3 minutes. Add zest, juice and rum; cool.

• Combine with kiwis and any combination of melon balls. Refrigerate until ready to serve.

Tarragon Chicken Salad

Cucumber Avocado Bisque

1 medium cucumber, peeled and seeded

½ medium avocado, peeled and pitted

3 green onions, chopped

1 cup chicken stock

1 cup sour cream

2 tablespoons fresh lemon juice

½ teaspoon salt

Paprika for garnish (optional)

Chopped fresh parsley for garnish (optional)

• Blend cucumber, avocado, onion, stock, sour cream, lemon juice and salt in a food processor for 10 to 15 seconds. Cover and chill.

• Serve in chilled mugs or soup bowls. Garnish with paprika or chopped fresh parsley, if desired.

Serves 6

3	pounds boneless, skinless chicken breasts
1	cup heavy cream
1	cup sour cream
1	cup mayonnaise

2	stalks celery, finely chopped
½	cup toasted walnuts
1	tablespoon dried tarragon or more to taste
	Salt and pepper to taste

• Preheat oven to 350°.

• Arrange chicken breasts in a single layer in a large baking pan. Spread evenly with cream season with salt and pepper. Bake 30 to 35 minutes, or until done. Remove from oven and coo

• Whisk sour cream and mayonnaise together.

• Shred meat and transfer to a bowl. Pour sour cream mixture over chicken. Add celery, walnuts, tarragon, salt and pepper to taste; toss well.

• Refrigerate, covered, at least 4 hours. Taste and correct seasoning before serving.

• Serve as a salad on a bed of greens or on a croissant as a sandwich.

Serves 6 to 8

Curried Chicken Salad

4	chicken breasts, cooked and cubed	1	(3-ounce) package cream cheese, softened
½	cup chopped celery	½	cup mayonnaise
½	cup chopped cashew nuts	¼	cup chutney
½	cup shredded carrots	¾	teaspoon curry powder
¼	cup sliced green onions	¼	teaspoon garlic salt

- Combine chicken, celery, cashews, carrots and onions.
- Mix cream cheese, mayonnaise, chutney, curry and garlic salt. Add to chicken and stir well. Refrigerate several hours or overnight.

Serves 6

Blue Cheese Potato Salad

8	potatoes	¼	teaspoon black pepper
2	tablespoons chopped parsley	8	ounces blue cheese, crumbled
3	green onions with tops, chopped	3	hard-cooked eggs, diced
2½	teaspoons salt		Bacon, cooked and crumbled, for garnish
1	cup sour cream		
½	cup slivered almonds, toasted		

- Peel potatoes. Cook in boiling water until tender. Cool and dice.
- In a large bowl, mix parsley, onion, salt, sour cream, almonds, pepper, cheese and eggs. Add potatoes and toss gently to coat.
- Garnish with bacon.

Serves 8

Quick Tomato Aspic

1 (6-ounce) package lemon-flavored gelatin

2 cups tomato juice, divided

1 tablespoon vinegar

1 tablespoon onion juice

1 cup chopped celery

Cooked shrimp (optional)

- Heat 1 cup tomato juice to boiling. Add gelatin and dissolve. Add remaining juice. Chill just until starts to set and add vinegar, onion juice and celery. Add shrimp, if desired. Chill overnight.

Serves 6

Citrus Poppy Seed Chicken Salad

Dressing

½ cup sugar	⅓ cup cider vinegar, divided
1 teaspoon dry mustard	1 cup vegetable oil
½ teaspoon salt	1 tablespoon poppy seeds
2 tablespoons grated onion	

- In a medium bowl, mix together sugar, mustard and salt. Stir in onion and 2 tablespoons vinegar; whisk until smooth. Gradually add oil and remaining vinegar, whisking constantly until smooth. Add poppy seeds. (May be made in a covered jar; shake well to blend.)

Salad

1 chicken, cooked and cut into ½-inch cubes, or 3 pounds chicken breasts, cooked and cut into 1-inch cubes	1 tablespoon fresh lemon juice
	Lettuce leaves for serving
1-2 firm, ripe mango, peeled, pitted and cut into ½-inch cubes	1 star fruit (carambola) cut horizontally into ¼-inch slices for garnish (optional)
1 (15-ounce) can Mandarin oranges, drained	½ cup slivered almonds, toasted, for garnish
1 avocado, peeled, pitted and cut into ½-inch cubes	

- Place chicken, mango and orange sections in a large bowl. Sprinkle avocado with lemon juice and add to bowl.

- Pour ½ cup of dressing over chicken mixture and toss gently but thoroughly. Add more dressing if salad seems dry.

- Line a serving platter with lettuce leaves. Mound salad on platter and garnish with slices of star fruit, if desired, and toasted almonds.

Variation: Another attractive presentation is to serve salad in hollowed out avocado shells.

Serves 6 to 8

Oriental Chicken and Rice Salad

Salad

1	(6-ounce) box long-grain and wild rice mix, with seasoning packet
4	chicken breasts, deboned
1	small onion, chopped
1	cup celery, chopped

¼	cup sesame oil, divided
1	(6-ounce) can whole salted almonds
1	(8-ounce) can sliced water chestnuts
	Handful raisins
	Soy sauce to taste
	Salt to taste

- Prepare rice according to package directions; drain and set aside.
- Marinate chicken in soy sauce and some of the sesame oil for 10 minutes.
- In a skillet, sauté chicken in marinade 20 minutes on low heat. Drain. Cool and dice chicken; set aside.
- Sauté onion and celery in small amount of sesame oil. Add chicken, almonds, water chestnuts and raisins. Salt to taste. Add soy sauce to taste.

Vinaigrette Dressing

5	tablespoons sugar
2	tablespoons sesame oil
2	teaspoons salt

¼	cup canola oil
6	tablespoons vinegar

- Combine sugar, sesame oil, salt, canola oil and vinegar in a jar with tight fitting lid. Shake to thoroughly blend dressing and pour over chicken mixture just before serving. Serve at room temperature.

Serves 6 to 8

Roquefort (Blue Cheese) Salad Dressing

1   cup mayonnaise
¼   cup buttermilk
½   cup sour cream
2-3 ounces blue cheese, crumbled

1   clove garlic, crushed or ¼ teaspoon
    garlic powder
    Salt to taste

- Whip mayonnaise, buttermilk and sour cream together until smooth. Add cheese, garlic and salt; mix well.
- Use as a dip for Zesty Chicken Strips or toss with mixed greens and chicken strips for a main dish.

Makes 2 cups

Zesty Chicken Strips

3 pounds boneless chicken breast halves

½ cup lemon juice

2 tablespoons soy sauce

1¼ teaspoons salt, divided

1 cup all-purpose flour

1 teaspoon pepper

½ teaspoon paprika

3 cups vegetable oil

- Cut chicken into 3 x 1-inch strips and place in a shallow dish. Combine lemon juice, soy sauce and ¾ teaspoon salt and pour over chicken. Cover dish and marinate 30 minutes.

- Combine flour, pepper, remaining ½ teaspoon salt and paprika. Dredge chicken pieces in flour mixture and fry in hot 375° oil until golden brown. Drain on paper towels.

Serves 8 to 10

Ginger Dressing

½   onion, minced
½   cup peanut oil (or whatever is on
    hand)
⅓   cup rice vinegar
2   tablespoons fresh ginger, minced
2   tablespoons minced celery
4   teaspoons soy sauce

3   teaspoons sugar
2   teaspoons lemon juice
2   tablespoons catsup
½   teaspoon minced garlic
½   teaspoon salt
¼   teaspoon black pepper

- In a blender, combine onion, oil, vinegar, ginger, celery, soy sauce, sugar, lemon juice, catsup, garlic, salt and pepper. Blend on high speed until all of ginger is well puréed.
- Keeps in refrigerator up to 2 weeks.

Makes 1½ cups

California Fruit Salad

Dressing

¼ cup mayonnaise	1 teaspoon lime juice
¼ cup sour cream	½ teaspoon lime zest
1 tablespoon honey	

- In medium bowl, combine mayonnaise, sour cream, honey, lime juice and zest. Cover and chill to blend flavors.

Salad

2 cantaloupes, cut in half crosswise and seeded	1 cup blueberries
2 cups honeydew melon, cut into 1-inch cubes	½ cup (2 ounces) crumbled blue cheese (optional)
1 cup sliced strawberries	

- In medium bowl, combine honeydew, strawberries and blueberries.
- To serve, fill each cantaloupe half with 1 cup mixed fruit. Sprinkle each with 2 tablespoons blue cheese, then drizzle each with 2 tablespoons dressing.

Serves 4

French Dressing

¾ cup sugar	4 tablespoons lemon juice
1 cup oil	⅔ cup grated onion
⅔ cup catsup	Salt
½ cup vinegar	

- Mix sugar, oil, catsup, vinegar, lemon juice, onion and salt until blended thoroughly.

Makes approximately 4 cups

Waldorf Coleslaw

6 cups shredded cabbage

2 cups chopped apple

½ cup raisins

¼ cup peanuts

½ cup mayonnaise, or more to taste

Salt and pepper to taste

• Combine cabbage, apple, raisins, peanuts, mayonnaise, salt and pepper. Add enough mayonnaise to moisten.

Serves 6

Grinders

Italian or French roll
Olive oil
Lettuce, shredded
Tomatoes, sliced
Onions, thinly sliced
Genoa salami, sliced

Capicola (Italian hot ham) or ham, sliced
Salt and pepper
Oregano
Provolone cheese, sliced

• Heat oven broiler.

• Slice roll in half lengthwise. Lay bread flat and drizzle with olive oil over inside surface. Top with meats, lettuce, tomatoes and onion.

• Salt and pepper vegetables to taste, sprinkle with oregano and additional olive oil. Place cheese on top.

• Leaving sandwich open, place on baking sheet and place about 8 inches away from broiler and cook until cheese is melted, not brown. Close sandwich to serve. If using a large loaf of bread, cut into individual portions.

Variation: Ham and cheese or a combination of cheeses is delicious as well.

Southwestern Chicken Spirals

1   (7-ounce) jar roasted red bell peppers
2   cups chopped cooked chicken
1   (8-ounce) package cream cheese, softened
1   (1-ounce) envelope Ranch-style buttermilk dressing mix
¼   cup chopped ripe olives
½   small onion, diced

1   (4½-ounce) can chopped green chiles, drained
2   tablespoons chopped fresh cilantro or 2 teaspoons dried
½   teaspoon black pepper
¼   cup pine nuts (optional)
8   (6-inch) flour tortillas

- Drain roasted peppers well, pressing between layers of paper towels to remove excess moisture; chop.
- In a large bowl, stir together roasted peppers, chicken, cream cheese, dressing mix, olives, onion, chiles, cilantro and pepper. Cover and chill at least 2 hours.
- Stir pine nuts, if desired, into chicken mixture. Spoon evenly over tortillas and roll up.
- Serve whole or cut in half and garnished with fresh cilantro for a luncheon.

Variation: This may also be used as an appetizer by slicing each roll into 5 slices.

Serves 8 to 10

Quick Fiesta Soup

1 medium onion, chopped

2 cloves garlic, minced

1 tablespoon oil

4 medium zucchini, grated

4 cups water

4 teaspoons low-salt chicken bouillon

2 (16-ounce) cans stewed tomatoes

2 (15-ounce) cans tomato sauce

2 (15.25-ounce) cans whole kernel corn, undrained

1½ teaspoons cumin

¼ teaspoon black pepper

Cheddar cheese

Tortilla chips

- In a large saucepan, sauté onion and garlic in oil. Add zucchini, water, bouillon, tomatoes, tomato sauce, corn, cumin and pepper. Cook until vegetables are tender.

- Sprinkle with Cheddar cheese and tortilla chips on top.

Serves 12

Stromboli

Great Combinations For Stromboli

• Pepperoni and sliced or grated mozzarella or provolone cheese; very greasy, but good!

• Pepper ham and cheese; rub dough with olive oil and sprinkle with onion powder

• Broccoli and grated Cheddar cheese; rub dough with oil and crushed garlic

• Spinach and grated Cheddar cheese; rub dough with oil and crushed garlic

• Sliced or crushed meat balls, a little sauce and shredded mozzarella cheese

• Roasted red peppers and grated mozzarella cheese; rub dough with oil and crushed garlic

1	loaf frozen bread dough	½	pound sliced cheese
½	pound sliced lunch meat		

• Follow instructions on bread dough package for quick thawing method or wrap tightly in plastic wrap and thaw in refrigerator.

• After dough is thawed, cut in half. Lightly flour a clean flat surface. Stretch out or roll dough, like for a pizza crust, to make a rectangle.

• Preheat oven to 375°.

• Layer ¼ pound of meat over dough and overlap ¼ pound of cheese over meat, covering entire area. Fold left end to middle then right end all the way over and pinch to seal.

• Place on cookie sheet sprayed with nonstick cooking spray. Two should fit on a large cookie sheet. Bake 20 to 30 minutes.

Serves 4

Tee Time Sandwich

1   large round loaf French bread, or any other shape
1   clove garlic, halved
1   teaspoon balsamic vinegar

1   tablespoon olive oil
    Salt and pepper to taste

- Cut bread in half and scoop out inside of bread halves. Rub with garlic on inside of each side and drizzle with vinegar, oil, salt and pepper.
- Layer with your choice of:

    Start and end with layers of tomato slices
    Crumbled soft cheese such as feta, Montrachet
    Sliced cucumber
    Roasted red pepper
    Grated carrots
    Sliced hard-boiled eggs

    Grilled tuna, swordfish or any meat of your choice
    Parboiled green beans
    Thinly sliced red onion
    Leaves of fresh basil or rosemary
    Dressing of your choice, in-between any layer mentioned above.

- Wrap sandwich tightly with aluminum foil and place on a plate with a heavy object on top for at least 1 hour, turning once and chill 6 to 8 hours.
- When ready to serve, slice into 6 wedges.

Serves 6

Vegetable Burritos

⅔ cup chopped onion
½ cup shredded carrot
1 clove garlic, crushed
1 tablespoon olive oil
1 (15-ounce) can black beans, rinsed and drained
1 (10-ounce) package frozen chopped broccoli, thawed and drained
1 (8-ounce) package frozen whole kernel corn, thawed and drained

1 (8-ounce) can tomato sauce
1 tablespoon chili powder
½ teaspoon salt
¼ teaspoon ground cumin
  Dash hot sauce
8 (9-inch) flour tortillas
8 ounces shredded Cheddar cheese
  Commercially prepared salsa
  Commercially prepared guacamole

- Sauté onion, carrot and garlic in hot oil in a large skillet over medium-high heat 2 minutes. Add beans, broccoli, corn, tomato sauce, chili powder, salt, cumin and hot sauce; bring to a boil. Reduce heat and simmer 5 minutes.

- Heat tortillas according to package directions.

- Spoon ½ cup vegetable mixture down center of each tortilla; top each with ¼ cup cheese. Fold bottom third of each tortilla over filling. Fold 1 side of tortilla in toward center and fold top over. Serve with salsa and guacamole.

Serves 4

Asparagus Sandwich Mix

1 (14½-ounce) can cut asparagus
1 teaspoon finely chopped onion
1 (8-ounce) package cream cheese, softened
3 tablespoons mayonnaise
½ cup finely chopped almonds

- Drain asparagus well in colander. Mash with fork or put into blender. Combine asparagus with onion, cream cheese, mayonnaise and almonds; mix well.
- Refrigerate overnight. Use as sandwich spread. Makes great finger sandwiches for parties.

Makes 2 cups

Homemade Mayonnaise

1 egg
½ teaspoon salt
½ teaspoon mustard
¼ teaspoon paprika
1 tablespoon vinegar
1 cup oil
1 tablespoon lemon juice

- In blender, combine egg, salt, mustard, paprika and vinegar. Start blending. Very gradually, add 1 cup oil while blending. Add lemon juice.

- Perfect on a fresh tomato sandwich on white bread.

Makes 1 cup

Grilled Reubens

Classic Thousand Island Dressing

1 cup mayonnaise

½ cup chili sauce

2 tablespoons salad olives

1 tablespoon chopped fresh parsley

1 tablespoon diced pimiento

2 teaspoons honey

½ teaspoon lemon juice

¼ teaspoon onion powder

12 capers

• Combine mayonnaise and chili sauce; mix well. Add olives, parsley, pimiento, honey, lemon juice, onion powder and capers; stir to blend well. Cover and chill at least 1 hour.

Makes 1¾ cups

2 cups canned sauerkraut, drained

¾ teaspoon caraway seeds

Classic Thousand Island Dressing (see accompanying recipe)

12 slices rye bread without caraway seeds, divided

6 slices pumpernickel bread

12 (1-ounce) slices Swiss cheese

2 pounds corned beef, thinly sliced (about 48 slices)

Butter or margarine, softened

6 pimiento-stuffed olives

• Combine sauerkraut and caraway seeds; set aside. Spread 1⅓ cups Classic Thousand Island Dressing over 1 side of 6 slices rye and 6 slices pumpernickel bread. Place 1 slice cheese over dressing on each slice bread. Layer sauerkraut mixture and corned beef evenly over cheese slices. Stack to make 6 (2-layer) sandwiches. Spread remaining 6 rye bread slices with remaining dressing; invert onto tops of sandwiches.

• Spread butter on outside of top slice of bread on each sandwich; invert sandwiches onto a hot griddle or skillet. Cook until bread is golden. Spread butter on ungrilled side of sandwiches; turn carefully and cook until bread is golden and cheese is slightly melted. Secure sandwiches with wooden picks, topped with olives. Serve warm.

Serves 6

Entrées

Travel on a winding mountain road through Hickory Nut Gorge, and you will soon find yourself by the tranquil waters of Lake Lure. Little do you realize as you look across the sparkling clear water that this lake only came into being in the last century. In the early 1900s Dr. Lucius Morse came to seek a restful refuge and a place to recover from his failing health. What he accomplished was so much more. Gazing at the roaring Rocky Broad River, he thought of the results a dam would make for this area. By 1926 the dam was completed and the lake was formed. Dr. Morse turned to his wife to find the appropriate name for the new lake and the story of Lake Lure began.

Over the years, the lake has seen generations enjoying this waterside retreat. Boating over a shimmering surface … young boys casting their first fishing lines … squeals of happy children splashing by the shore. Lake Lure continues to entice couples and families to its waters. Whether you are wishing to make a mouthwatering meal to enjoy on the deck or "munchies" for a day on the water, this next section is sure to provide something to satisfy your family's cravings!

Salmon Just Right

4	salmon fillets	1	tablespoon Dijon mustard
2	tablespoons olive oil		

- One hour before serving time, very lightly brush fish with olive oil on both sides then coat both sides with mustard. Cover and chill.
- Twenty minutes before serving time, place oven rack 2 tiers below oven broiler. Turn on broiler and place an ungreased, shallow baking pan under broiler. Heat pan ten minutes then remove from oven and place salmon fillets on hot pan, skin side down.
- Place under broiler and cook 10 minutes. Fish is done when pieces flake easily with a fork.

Serves 4

Note: Delicious served with roasted red and yellow bell peppers and tossed with a tablespoon of both balsamic vinegar and olive oil.

Summer Salsa

1 cup chopped
fresh tomato

1 medium avocado,
chopped

1 large clove garlic,
crushed

2 tablespoons
balsamic vinegar

2 tablespoons olive oil

½ cup whole
kernel corn

¼ cup chopped
green onions

¼ cup chopped fresh
cilantro

Salt and pepper
to taste

1 teaspoon fresh
lime juice

- Combine tomato, avocado, garlic, vinegar, oil, corn, onion, cilantro, salt, pepper and lime juice. Allow to stand to let flavors meld for 30 minutes. Great as a side dish for fish.

Makes 3 cups

Broad River Salmon

Dill Sauce

1 cup non-fat yogurt

2 tablespoons low-fat
mayonnaise

½ teaspoon brown
mustard

1 tablespoon snipped
fresh dill

• In a small bowl,
combine yogurt,
mayonnaise and mustard
until thoroughly mixed.
Stir in dill. Cover and
refrigerate at least 1 hour
to blend flavors.

Makes approximately 1½ cups

2	(6-ounce) salmon fillets	2	teaspoons olive oil
	Salt and freshly ground black pepper to taste	1½	tablespoons balsamic vinegar
		1½	tablespoons honey

• Preheat oven to 400°. Pat salmon dry and season with salt and pepper.

• Heat oil in skillet over medium-high heat. Add salmon (skin side up). Do not turn it for 2 minutes. (If salmon sticks to pan, it is not properly seared.) Turn and cook until lightly browned and crisp - about 2 minutes.

• While salmon is cooking, whisk vinegar and honey together. Drizzle top of each fillet with glaze. Transfer to oven and finish cooking to desired doneness (approximately 10 to 15 minutes).

• Place salmon on plates and drizzle with remaining glaze.

Serves 2

Baked Garlic Salmon

---

1 ½ pounds salmon fillets
Olive oil
3-5 cloves garlic, crushed (depending on size of cloves)
Salt and pepper to taste

5 sprigs of fresh dill, 3 chopped (dried dill is fine for cooking fish, not for garnish)
2 chopped green onions
3-5 very thin slices lemon for garnish (optional)

- Preheat oven to 450°.

- Spray 2 large pieces of aluminum foil with nonstick cooking spray. Place salmon fillet on top of one piece of foil. Rub with olive oil and garlic. Salt and pepper to taste. Top salmon with onion and chopped dill.

- Arrange lemon slices on top along with 2 sprigs of fresh dill. Cover with second piece of foil and pinch foil together to seal tightly.

- Place on baking sheet or 13 x 9 x 2-inch pan. Bake for 20 to 25 minutes or until salmon flakes easily.

Serves 4

Barbecue Roasted Salmon

¼ cup pineapple juice
2 tablespoons fresh lemon juice
4 (6-ounce) salmon fillets
2 tablespoons brown sugar
4 teaspoons chili powder
2 teaspoons grated lemon zest

¾ teaspoon ground cumin
½ teaspoon salt
¼ teaspoon ground cinnamon
Nonstick cooking spray
Lemon slices (optional)

- Combine pineapple juice, lemon juice and salmon in a resealable plastic bag, seal and marinate in refrigerator 1 hour, turning occasionally.

- Preheat oven to 400°.

- Remove fish from bag, discard marinade. Combine brown sugar, chili powder, lemon zest, cumin, salt and cinnamon in a bowl. Rub over fish, place in an 11x7 x 2-inch baking dish coated with nonstick cooking spray. Bake for 12 minutes or until fish flakes easily when tested with a fork. Serve with lemon slices, if desired.

Serves 4

Olympian Fish

1	(12-ounce) package frozen spinach soufflé, thawed
½	cup crumbled feta cheese
½	cup coarsely chopped roasted red peppers

½	teaspoon dried oregano
2	(6-ounce) halibut, cod or tilapia fillets, skinned
¼	teaspoon lemon pepper

- Preheat oven to 350°.

- Combine spinach soufflé, feta cheese, red peppers and oregano.

- Place fish in a baking dish and sprinkle with lemon pepper. Spread spinach mixture over fish.

- Bake for 30 minutes or until fish is done.

Serves 2

Stuffed Sole Fillets

2½	cups small white bread cubes
1	(2-ounce) jar diced pimientos, drained
2	green onions or 1 small onion, minced
3	tablespoons chopped parsley, divided
2	medium carrots, peeled and shredded

6	tablespoons butter, melted, divided
¼	teaspoon salt
⅛	teaspoon black pepper
6	large sole fillets (about 2 pounds)
	Paprika to taste

- Preheat oven to 375°.

- In bowl, combine bread cubes, pimiento, onion, 2 tablespoons parsley, carrots, 4 tablespoons butter, ¼ teaspoon salt and ⅛ teaspoon pepper; mix well. Sprinkle one side of fillets lightly with salt and pepper.

- Divide stuffing onto fillets and, starting from small end, roll tightly. Put seam side down in 9 x 9 x 2-inch baking dish. Drizzle with remaining 2 tablespoons butter.

- Bake 30 minutes or until fish flakes easily with fork. Sprinkle with remaining 1 tablespoon parsley and paprika.

Serves 6

Easy Baked Fish

2 tablespoons plus 4 teaspoons butter, divided
Salt and freshly ground pepper to taste
2 tablespoons finely chopped shallots
2 pounds fish fillets (fluke, flounder or sole)
½ cup dry white wine

2 teaspoons Dijon mustard
6 tablespoons fine fresh bread crumbs
¼ cup finely chopped parsley
Lemon wedges

- Preheat oven to 400°.
- Grease a 13 x 9 x 2-inch baking dish (large enough to fit all fish in one layer) with 2 tablespoons butter. Sprinkle with salt, pepper and shallots.
- Arrange fish over shallots and sprinkle with ¼ cup of wine. Blend remaining wine with mustard and brush on top of fish. Sprinkle with crumbs and dot with 4 teaspoons butter.
- Bake 5 minutes. Turn oven to broil and place dish under broiler until fish flakes easily when tested with a fork. Sprinkle with chopped parsley, garnish with lemon and serve.

Serves 4 to 6

Trout Amandine

2	cups milk	¾	cup sliced almonds
2	teaspoons salt, divided	2	tablespoons lemon juice
¼	teaspoon hot sauce	2	teaspoons Worcestershire sauce
6	(8- to 10-ounce) trout fillets	¼	cup chopped fresh parsley
¾	cup all-purpose flour		Parsley for garnish
½	teaspoon black pepper		Red bell pepper for garnish
1¼	cups butter or margarine, divided		Hot cooked couscous
1	tablespoon olive oil		

- Stir together milk, 1 teaspoon salt and hot sauce in a 13 x 9 x 2-inch baking dish. Add fillets, turning to coat. Cover and chill 2 hours.
- Combine flour and black pepper in a shallow dish.
- Melt ¼ cup butter in a large skillet over medium heat; add oil. Remove fillets from marinade, discarding marinade. Dredge fillets in flour mixture. Add to skillet; cook 2 minutes on each side or until golden. Remove to a serving platter and keep warm.
- Combine remaining 1 cup butter and almonds in a saucepan and cook over medium heat until lightly browned.
- Stir in lemon juice, Worcestershire and remaining 1 teaspoon salt. Cook 2 minutes. Remove from heat and stir in chopped parsley; pour over fillets. Serve immediately over couscous.

Serves 6

Note: You may prepare fillets and sauce up to 45 minutes before serving. Heat oven to 250°; turn oven off. Place cooked fillets in warm oven. Cook sauce over low heat until warm, and drizzle over fillets just before serving.

Shrimp Bisque Casserole

2 pounds shrimp (or crabmeat or mixture of both)
3 slices soft bread, crusts removed and cubed
1 cup evaporated milk
1¼ cups mayonnaise
3 hard-cooked eggs, grated
1 teaspoon chopped onion

1 tablespoon minced parsley
⅛ teaspoon black pepper
1 teaspoon monosodium glutamate (MSG)
2 tablespoons sherry
½ cup herb-seasoned stuffing, crushed
2 tablespoons butter

- Preheat oven to 350°.
- Combine all ingredients except butter and stuffing. Place in a greased casserole. Sprinkle with stuffing and dot with butter.
- Bake 20 minutes or until thoroughly heated and bubbly.

Serves 6, generously

Shrimp and Scallops Stroganoff

1	pound uncooked jumbo or large shrimp, peeled and deveined	2	tablespoons all-purpose flour
1	pound sea scallops	⅛	teaspoon black pepper
½	pound white mushrooms, sliced	1	cup chicken broth
3	tablespoons butter, divided	1	cup sour cream
3	tablespoons dry sherry	2	teaspoons minced parsley for garnish

- About 45 minutes before serving: Rinse shrimp with running cold water. Rinse scallops to remove sand from crevices. Pat shrimp and scallops dry with paper towels.

- Heat 2 tablespoons butter in a heavy, large skillet over medium-high heat. Cook shrimp and scallops, stirring frequently, until shrimp turn pink and scallops are tender, about 5 minutes. With slotted spoon, remove shrimp and scallops to a bowl.

- To drippings in skillet, add remaining 1 tablespoon hot butter. Add mushrooms and sherry; cook, stirring frequently, until mushrooms are tender.

- In a cup, stir flour, pepper and broth until blended. Add to mushroom mixture and cook, stirring constantly, until sauce boils and thickens slightly. Reduce heat to low; stir in sour cream until blended. Return shrimp and scallops to skillet and cook over low heat, stirring constantly, until shrimp and scallops are hot. Do not boil!

- Pour mixture into serving bowl; garnish with minced parsley. Serve over rice or noodles.

Serves 6

Oven-Baked Coconut Shrimp with Pineapple Salsa

28   large shrimp (about 1½ pounds), peeled, deveined, tails intact

⅓   cup cornstarch

¼   teaspoon salt

½-¾   teaspoon cayenne pepper

3   large egg whites

1½   cups flaked sweetened coconut

Nonstick cooking spray

Pineapple Salsa (see accompanying recipe)

- Preheat oven to 400°. Rinse shrimp in cold water; drain well on paper towels.

- Combine cornstarch, salt and cayenne pepper in shallow dish; stir with whisk. Place egg whites in medium bowl and beat with electric mixer at medium-high speed until frothy, about 2 minutes. Place coconut in shallow dish.

- Coat baking sheet with nonstick cooking spray. Working with 1 shrimp at a time: dredge in cornstarch mixture, dip in egg white, then dredge in coconut, pressing gently with fingers. Place shrimp on prepared sheet. Repeat with remaining shrimp. Lightly coat shrimp with cooking spray.

- Bake 20 minutes or until shrimp are done, turning after 10 minutes. Serve with Pineapple Salsa.

Serves 4

Note: It is intended that this shrimp be eaten with a fork.

Pineapple Salsa

1 cup finely chopped fresh pineapple

⅓ cup chopped red onion

¼ cup finely chopped fresh cilantro

¼ cup pineapple preserves (or apricot-pineapple preserves)

1 tablespoon finely chopped, seeded fresh jalapeño

1½ tablespoons fresh lime juice

¼ teaspoon ground black pepper

- Gently toss pineapple, onion, cilantro, preserves, jalapeño, lime juice and black pepper together until well blended.

Shrimp and Scallop Coquilles Over Angel Hair Pasta

1 (16-ounce) package angel hair pasta
1 pound fresh shrimp, peeled
½ pound scallops
3 tablespoons butter
1 cup milk
1 tablespoon basil
1 teaspoon thyme

½ teaspoon cayenne pepper
Cornstarch
½ cup (2 ounces) grated Parmesan cheese
1 cup (4 ounces) shredded mozzarella cheese
Parsley for garnish
1 slice lemon for garnish

- Preheat oven to 375°.
- Prepare angel hair according to package directions, cook until al dente. While pasta cooks, prepare sauce.
- Sauté shrimp and scallops in butter.
- Add milk, basil, thyme and cayenne. Bring to a simmer. Stir in cornstarch to thicken to preference.
- Drain pasta. Place in 2-quart casserole dish. Layer sauce on pasta and sprinkle with cheeses.
- Bake until cheese is golden. Garnish with parsley and lemon twist.

Serves 4 to 6

Shrimp and Sausage Jambalaya

1 pound smoked sausage, thinly sliced	1½ teaspoons thyme
3 tablespoons olive oil	2 bay leaves
⅔ cup chopped bell pepper	2 teaspoons oregano
2 cloves garlic, minced	1 tablespoon Creole seasoning
¾ cup chopped fresh parsley	½ teaspoon salt
1 cup chopped celery	½ teaspoon cayenne pepper
2 (16-ounce) cans diced tomatoes, undrained	½ teaspoon black pepper
2 cups chicken broth	2 cups long-grain converted rice, washed
1 cup chopped green onions	3 pounds raw shrimp, peeled

- In a 4-quart heavy pot, sauté sausage; remove with slotted spoon. Add oil to pan drippings and sauté bell pepper, garlic, parsley and celery 5 minutes.

- Add tomatoes and liquid, broth and onion. Stir in thyme, bay leaves, oregano, Creole seasoning, salt, cayenne pepper and black pepper. Add rice which has been washed and rinsed three times. Add sausage and cook 30 minutes, covered, over low heat, stirring occasionally.

- After most liquid has been absorbed by rice, add shrimp and cook until pink. Transfer mixture to an oblong baking dish. Bake approximately 25 minutes until heated through.

Serves 12 to 14

Note: Be sure rice is not crunchy after 30 minutes of cooking. If not done, add more chicken broth and continue cooking until done.

Seashore Delight

1	cup regular rice, uncooked		1	cup chopped celery
1	cup sliced fresh mushrooms		1	cup mayonnaise
	Butter		½	teaspoon salt
1	pound premium white crabmeat		¼	teaspoon black pepper
1	pound shrimp, cooked and peeled		1	cup half & half
½	cup bell pepper, chopped		1	tablespoon Worcestershire sauce
½	cup chopped onion			Buttered bread crumbs
1	(2-ounce) jar diced pimiento, drained			

- Preheat oven to 350°.

- Prepare rice according to package directions

- Sauté mushrooms in small amount of butter until tender.

- Combine crabmeat, shrimp, bell pepper, onion, pimiento, celery and mushrooms.

- Blend mayonnaise, salt, pepper, half & half, Worcestershire sauce and rice. Fold in seafood mixture and combine.

- Spread mixture in buttered 3-quart casserole dish. Sprinkle with bread crumbs.

- Bake 30 minutes.

Serves 8

Sautéed Shrimp, Sausage and Grits

1	pound bulk pork sausage		Oregano to taste
1	teaspoon clarified butter		Thyme to taste
20	shrimp, peeled and deveined	1	tablespoon bourbon
3	tablespoons chopped scallions	2	tablespoons butter
	Salt and pepper to taste	2	cups cooked grits
	Basil to taste		

- Shape sausage into nickel-sized balls. Sauté sausage balls in clarified butter in skillet until nearly cooked.
- Add shrimp, scallions, salt, pepper, basil, oregano and thyme. Toss and cook for approximately 1 minute. Remove from skillet and pour over hot grits.
- Deglaze skillet with bourbon and ignite. After flames subside, add 2 tablespoons butter, stir and pour over shrimp, sausage and grits. Serve immediately.

Serves 4

Shrimp Scampi Bake

1	cup butter	1	tablespoon chopped fresh parsley (or 1½ teaspoons dried)
2	tablespoons Dijon mustard		
1	tablespoon fresh lemon juice	2	pounds medium raw shrimp, shelled, deveined and tails removed
1	tablespoon chopped garlic (3 to 4 cloves)		

- Preheat oven to 450°.
- In a small saucepan over medium heat, combine butter, mustard, lemon juice, garlic and parsley. When butter melts completely, remove from heat.
- Arrange shrimp in a shallow baking dish. Pour butter mixture over shrimp.
- Bake 12 to 15 minutes or until shrimp are pink and opaque. Serve over rice.

Serves 4

To Clarify Butter

1 pound butter

- Cut butter into small pieces and place into a saucepan over moderate heat. When butter has melted, let it boil slowly, watching that it does not foam up over rim of pan.
- Simmer a few minutes and remove from heat and cool.
- Strain through lined colander into a jar. Keeps for months in refrigerator in closed container.

Makes 1½ cups

Oven Roasted Cajun Shrimp with Corn-on-the-Cob

Shrimp Cocktail Sauce

¾ cup chili sauce

¼ cup fresh lemon juice

1-2 tablespoons prepared horseradish

1 teaspoon minced onion

2 teaspoons Worcestershire sauce

4 drops hot sauce

Dash salt

• In a small bowl, combine chili sauce, lemon juice, horseradish, onion, Worcestershire, hot sauce and salt. Chill thoroughly.

Makes 1 cup

8	ears corn		2	teaspoons black pepper
4-5	pounds large shrimp		2	cloves garlic, minced
1	cup butter		2	tablespoons dried oregano
¼	cup olive oil			Cayenne pepper to taste
¼	cup Worcestershire sauce		½	teaspoon hot sauce
¼	cup soy sauce		4	lemons, sliced
2	teaspoons salt			

• Preheat oven to 500°.

• Boil corn in water for 5 minutes. Drain and cut ears in half. Place fresh shrimp and corn into a large 4-inch deep roasting pan.

• Cut butter into 1-inch slices, placing on top of shrimp and corn.

• Combine oil, Worcestershire, soy sauce, salt, pepper, garlic, oregano, cayenne pepper and hot sauce in a small bowl and pour over shrimp and corn. Top with lemon slices.

• Bake 8 to 10 minutes or until shrimp turn pink, basting and turning shrimp often.

Serves 10 to 12

Creamy Cocktail Sauce

1	cup mayonnaise		½	teaspoon Worcestershire sauce
1	teaspoon lemon juice		½	teaspoon red pepper sauce
1	teaspoon curry powder		¼	cup chili sauce
½	teaspoon finely minced onion			Salt and pepper to taste

• Combine mayonnaise, lemon juice, curry, onion, Worcestershire, pepper sauce, chili sauce, salt and pepper and store in refrigerator, covered, until ready to serve.

Southern Comfort

2-3 pounds large shrimp, peeled

Sauce

3	sticks butter	2	teaspoons salt
2	tablespoons lemon juice	1	tablespoon black pepper
1	teaspoon hot sauce, or to taste	¾	cup Worcestershire sauce
2-4	cloves garlic, crushed		

- Preheat oven to 400°.
- Melt butter in a saucepan. Add lemon juice, hot sauce, garlic, salt, pepper and Worcestershire and stir well. Arrange shrimp in single layer in a baking dish. Pour sauce over shrimp.
- Bake 15 minutes, turning once. Depending upon size of shrimp, some may take a little longer.
- Serve with lots of crusty bread for dipping in sauce.

Serves 4 for dinner (approximately ½ pound per person) or many as an appetizer.

Linguine with Shrimp and Feta Cheese

2 tablespoons butter
1½ pounds large shrimp, peeled
8 ounces linguine pasta
2 (10-ounce) cans diced tomatoes with green chiles
2 (14½-ounce) cans stewed tomatoes

¾ cup crumbled feta cheese
5 cloves garlic, minced
Oregano to taste
Basil to taste

- Sauté shrimp in a large skillet with butter. Set aside on warm.

- In a large pot, stir together tomatoes with chiles and stewed tomatoes, minced garlic, dash of basil and oregano. Bring to a simmer.

- In a large pot, boil water with a drop of olive oil and add linguine. Drain when fully cooked.

- Three minutes before serving, add feta cheese to tomato mixture. Allow to melt throughout while stirring.

- Add shrimp to mixture. Serve shrimp and sauce over linguine immediately.

Serves 4

Spicy Pasta and Shrimp

4	tablespoons butter	½	cup dry white wine
½	cup chopped green onions	8	ounces linguine, cooked
2	cloves garlic, minced	⅔	cup freshly grated Parmesan cheese
2	tablespoons Cajun or Creole seasoning	1-2	teaspoons dried crushed red pepper
1	pound fresh, medium shrimp, peeled and deveined	⅓	cup chopped fresh parsley
1	cup whipping cream		

- Melt butter in a large skillet; add green onions and garlic and sauté until tender. Stir in Cajun seasoning and cook, stirring constantly, 1 minute.

- Stir in shrimp and whipping cream; reduce heat, and simmer 3 minutes, stirring often. Stir in wine; simmer 3 minutes, stirring occasionally.

- Add linguine, Parmesan cheese, and crushed red pepper; cook, stirring gently, until thoroughly heated. Stir in chopped parsley; serve immediately.

Serves 4

Carolina Crab Cakes

1	egg	1	pound fresh crabmeat, cleaned and drained
2	tablespoons mayonnaise	3	tablespoons finely chopped fresh parsley
½	teaspoon dry mustard	¼	cup bread crumbs
⅛	teaspoon ground cayenne pepper	1	cup vegetable oil
¼	teaspoon hot sauce	1	lemon, cut into wedges
½	teaspoon salt		Tartar sauce
½	teaspoon black pepper		

- Beat egg lightly with whisk. Add mayonnaise, mustard, cayenne, hot sauce, salt and pepper until mixture is smooth. Add crabmeat, parsley and bread crumbs, toss with fork.

- Divide mixture into 8 equal portions and shape into 2 to 2½-inch circles. Wrap in waxed paper and chill for 30 minutes.

- Deep fry crab cakes in vegetable oil, 4 at a time until golden brown. Drain on paper towels and serve with lemon wedges and tartar sauce.

Serves 6

Chesapeake Crab Cakes

1 pound backfin crabmeat
½ cup soft bread crumbs
1 tablespoon minced onion
1 tablespoon finely chopped bell pepper
1 tablespoon chopped fresh parsley
¼ cup mayonnaise
1 egg
2 teaspoons white wine Worcestershire sauce

2 teaspoons lemon juice
1 teaspoon prepared mustard
½ teaspoon salt
¼ teaspoon ground white pepper
Vegetable oil for frying (optional)
Tartar Sauce (see accompanying recipe)

- Pick out and discard any shell or cartilage from crabmeat. Flake with fork. Place crabmeat in medium bowl. Add bread crumbs, onion, bell pepper and parsley; set aside.

- Mix mayonnaise, egg, Worcestershire, lemon juice, mustard, salt and white pepper in a small bowl. Stir well to combine. Pour mayonnaise mixture over crabmeat mixture. Gently mix so large lumps will not be broken. Shape mixture into 6 large cakes (¾-inch thick) or 36 bite-sized cakes.

- To Pan Fry: Pour enough oil into 12-inch skillet to cover bottom. Heat oil over medium-high heat until hot. Add crab cakes; fry 10 minutes for large cakes or 6 minutes for bite-sized cakes or until cakes are lightly browned on bottom. Using spatula, carefully turn halfway through cooking without breaking cakes.

- To Broil: Preheat broiler. Place crab cakes on broiler pan. Broil 4 to 6 inches below heat 10 minutes for large cakes or 6 minutes for bite-sized cakes until cakes are lightly browned on surface, turn halfway through cooking.

Serves 6

Sun-Dried Tomato Tartar Sauce

1 cup mayonnaise
2 tablespoons dill relish
1 clove garlic, minced
1 teaspoon fresh lemon juice
1 teaspoon prepared horseradish
2-3 dashes ground red pepper
3 tablespoons sun-dried tomatoes, packed in oil

- Combine mayonnaise, relish, garlic, lemon juice, horseradish and red pepper in a small bowl. Drain sun-dried tomatoes and pat dry with paper towels. Slice tomatoes lengthwise into thin strips and cut in half. Fold tomatoes into mayonnaise mixture.

Makes 1 cup

Risotto with Chicken and Caramelized Onions

4   tablespoons olive oil, divided
1   onion, coarsely chopped
¼   cup balsamic vinegar
7   cups unsalted chicken broth
1½ cups uncooked Arborio rice
¼   cup dry white wine

2   tablespoons chopped fresh thyme
2   tablespoons unsalted butter
2   cups chopped, cooked chicken or turkey breast
    Salt and pepper to taste
    Freshly grated Parmigiano-Reggiano or Pecorino
        Romano cheese

- Heat 2 tablespoons of oil in a medium saucepan over medium heat. Stir in onion and sauté 15 to 20 minutes, or until dark golden brown. Remove from heat, stir in balsamic vinegar and set aside.

- Meanwhile, heat broth in a saucepan and keep hot over low heat. Heat remaining oil in a separate large skillet over medium heat. Stir in rice and mix well. Cook about 2 minutes, then pour in wine. Cook, stirring constantly, until wine is almost completely reduced. Add just enough hot broth to barely cover rice.

- Cook, still over medium heat, stirring constantly, until the broth has been absorbed almost completely. Add more broth as the liquid is absorbed, continually stirring. Continue cooking and stirring the rice, adding broth a bit at a time, until rice is tender, but still firm to the bite. It is not absolutely necessary to add all the broth, only enough to cook until al dente. The total cooking time for risotto is about 20 to 25 minutes.

- Stir in reserved onion mixture and allow to heat through. Remove from heat and stir in thyme, butter and chicken. Season with salt and pepper to taste, and garnish each serving with freshly grated cheese.

Serves 4

Chicken Freedom

2	cups fresh bread crumbs		2	cloves garlic, chopped
1	cup grated Parmesan cheese		1½	tablespoons Dijon mustard
1	tablespoon salt		1½	tablespoons Worcestershire sauce
½	cup fresh chopped parsley		8	boneless, skinless chicken breasts
¾	pound butter, melted		10	ounces Cheddar cheese, sliced

- Preheat oven to 350°.

- Combine bread crumbs, Parmesan cheese, salt and parsley in a mixing bowl. In another bowl, combine butter, garlic, mustard and Worcestershire.

- Place small amount of cheese in center of each chicken breast. Roll; secure with string (or use raw spaghetti as a toothpick-fastener because it will cook and be easier to work with than string). Dip chicken in butter then crumb mixture. Pour remaining butter over chicken.

- Bake, uncovered, 1 hour. May be frozen before or after cooking.

Serves 8

Salsa Couscous Chicken

¼ cup slivered almonds
1-2 tablespoons olive oil
2 cloves garlic, minced
8 chicken thighs, trimmed
2 cups salsa, any kind, mild or medium

½ cup water
4 tablespoons currants
2 tablespoons honey
1½ teaspoons ground cinnamon
4 cups cooked couscous

- Preheat oven to 350°.

- In a large oven-proof skillet with lid, sauté almonds in oil until golden and remove almonds. Add garlic and chicken, browning over medium-high heat, 4 to 5 minutes.

- Combine salsa, water, currants, honey and cinnamon and add to chicken. Bake, covered, at least 1 hour; however, the longer the better. Add almonds and serve over couscous.

Serves 4

Note: Can also bake in a serving pan instead of skillet. It's even better doubling the amounts of the sauce ingredients for a saucier dish.

Chicken with Lime Butter

---

6 boneless, skinless chicken breasts
Salt
Black pepper
1 tablespoon oil

Juice of 1 lime
8 tablespoons butter
½ teaspoon chives
½ teaspoon dill weed

- Sprinkle chicken with salt and pepper. In a skillet, sauté chicken in oil on both sides until lightly browned and cooked through. Remove to serving platter and keep warm.

- Add lime juice to skillet and cook over low heat until it begins to bubble.

- Add butter and stir until it becomes opaque and forms a thicker sauce. Stir in chives and dill. Serve over chicken.

Serves 6

Spicy Ginger and Orange Chicken with Broccoli

2 tablespoons vegetable oil, divided
4 (6-ounce) boneless, skinless chicken breasts, cut into thin strips
½ small onion, diced
1 pound broccoli, cut into florets
3 tablespoons cornstarch
2 tablespoons fresh ginger, minced
1 teaspoon grated orange zest

½ teaspoon ground red pepper
1 teaspoon dark sesame oil
2 cloves garlic, minced
½ cup chicken broth
¼ cup orange marmalade
2 large oranges, peeled, sectioned and coarsely chopped
Cooked rice

- Heat wok, add 1 tablespoon oil and sauté chicken until done. Remove from pan and keep warm.

- Add 1 tablespoon oil to wok and sauté onion and broccoli until crisp-tender. Mix together cornstarch, ginger, orange zest, red pepper, sesame oil, garlic and marmalade, stirring until cornstarch, broth and marmalade dissolve.

- Add chicken back to wok with vegetables and add sauce. Stir until thickened and add oranges. Serve immediately over rice.

Serves 4

Chicken Karma

2 teaspoons curry
1 teaspoon ginger
2 teaspoons chili powder
1 teaspoon garlic powder
1 teaspoon salt

2 tablespoons olive oil
4 boneless, skinless chicken breasts, cut into strips
1 (8-ounce) carton sour cream
1 cup milk
Cooked rice

- In a bowl, mix curry, ginger, chili powder, garlic powder and salt together. Add to a large skillet with oil and simmer on low 5 minutes to allow spices to blend.

- Add strips of chicken and toss until covered with spices. Cook chicken approximately 6 minutes on each side on medium to medium-high heat.

- When chicken is cooked, add sour cream and milk. Cover until ready to serve. Serve over rice.

Serves 4 to 6

Slow Cooker Rosemary Chicken

6   medium red potatoes, halved
3   medium carrots, sliced
2   medium onions, cut into wedges
1   teaspoon salt

½   teaspoon black pepper
2-4 sprigs fresh rosemary
1   (3- to 3½-pound) whole chicken
½-1 cup fat-free chicken broth

- In a 4- or 5-quart slow cooker, place potatoes, carrots, onions, salt and pepper; mix well. Tuck rosemary sprigs under skin of chicken breast. Place in cooker. Pour ½ cup broth over top.
- Cover and cook on low 7 to 9 hours or on high for 3½ to 5 hours. (If cooking on high, use 1 cup broth). Remove chicken and discard skin.
- Place on large serving platter and surround with vegetables.

Serves 4

Jalapeño Chicken

¾   cup (3 ounces) shredded Monterrey Jack cheese
½   cup mayonnaise, divided
¼   cup sour cream
2   tablespoons chopped, fresh cilantro or parsley

1   tablespoon minced pickled jalapeño pepper
½   teaspoon minced garlic
3   whole boneless, skinless chicken breasts, halved
   Lettuce leaves, for serving

- In a small bowl combine cheese, ¼ cup mayonnaise, sour cream, cilantro, jalapeño and garlic; set aside.
- Between 2 sheets of waxed paper, pound chicken to ¼-inch thick. Brush both sides of chicken with remaining mayonnaise.
- Heat a large skillet over medium-high heat; add chicken. Cook, turning once, 4 minutes or until lightly browned. Place on rack in broiler pan. Spread cheese mixture onto each chicken breast.
- Broil 6 inches from heat for 3 to 4 minutes or until topping begins to brown.
- Serve chicken on lettuce.

Serves 6

Creamy Chicken Enchiladas

1	tablespoon butter or margarine	3½	cups cooked, chopped chicken breast
1	medium onion, chopped	8	(8-inch) flour tortillas
1	(4½-ounce) can chopped green chiles, drained	2	(8-ounce) packages shredded Monterey Jack cheese
1	(8-ounce) package cream cheese, cut into pieces and softened	2	cups whipping cream or half & half

- Preheat oven to 350°.
- Melt butter over medium heat; add onion and sauté 5 minutes. Add chiles; sauté 1 minute. Stir in cream cheese and chicken; cook, stirring constantly, until cream cheese melts.
- Spoon 2 to 3 tablespoons chicken mixture down center of each tortilla. Roll up tortillas and place, seam side down, in a lightly greased 13 x 9 x 2-inch baking dish.
- Sprinkle with Monterey Jack cheese and drizzle with whipping cream. Bake 45 minutes.

Serves 4 to 6

Chicken Clarisse

4	cups chicken breasts (bone in, skinned)	½	small onion, minced
1	cup apricot preserves	2	tablespoons soy sauce
½	cup barbecue sauce	2	cloves garlic, crushed and minced
			Salt and pepper to taste

- Preheat oven to 350°.
- Place chicken into a greased 13 x 9 x 2-inch baking dish. Combine preserves, barbecue sauce, onion, soy sauce, garlic, salt and pepper. Pour mixture over chicken. Bake 1 hour or until done.

Rainy Day Bar-B-Que Chicken

1 chicken, cut up, or any combination of cut-up bone-in chicken

1 (18-ounce) bottle prepared barbecue sauce, any kind

- Preheat oven to 325°.
- Place chicken in a 13 x 9 x 2-inch casserole, pour sauce over chicken. Cover tightly with aluminum foil.
- Bake 2 hours, uncover and bake 30 additional minutes.

Note: The longer this chicken is cooked, the more tender it becomes. More chicken can be used but use same amount of barbecue sauce.

Serves 4

Chicken Cranberry Bake

1	(6-ounce) box long-grain and wild rice with herb seasoning	¾	cup butter or margarine, divided
1	(16-ounce) bag frozen French-style green beans	½	cup chopped onion
1½	cups fresh cranberries or 2 (16-ounce) cans whole berry cranberry sauce	1	cup chopped celery
8	boneless skinless chicken breast halves	1	cup sliced mushrooms
	Paprika	½	cup slivered almonds
1	cup freshly grated Parmesan cheese	1	cup dry white wine

- Preheat oven to 350°.
- Prepare rice according to package directions.
- Cook green beans in small amount of boiling water for 4 to 5 minutes; drain.
- If using canned cranberry sauce, drain in colander until most of liquid is drained, leaving berries.
- Sprinkle chicken with paprika. Roll in cheese.
- Melt ½ cup butter in large skillet. Add onion, celery and mushrooms; sauté until soft. Stir in rice and cranberries.
- Place green beans and almonds in shallow 3-quart casserole dish. Place breasts on top in single layer in the center. Spoon rice mixture around edge of casserole. Pour wine over all. Dot chicken with ¼ cup butter. (May be prepared ahead to this point and refrigerated.)
- Bake 45 to 50 minutes.

Serves 6 to 8

Thai Chicken Stir Fry

1   cup Jasmine rice or converted rice
1   (14-ounce) can of Thai coconut milk, divided
1   cup water
½   teaspoon salt
3   tablespoons peanut butter
2   tablespoons soy sauce

1   tablespoon chili garlic paste or sauce
2   tablespoons dark sesame oil
2   boneless, skinless chicken breasts, sliced
3   green onions, cut diagonally
1   red bell pepper, cut into thin strips

- Cook rice in combination of 1 cup coconut milk, 1 cup water and ½ teaspoon salt as directed on package (20 minutes or until liquid is absorbed).

- Whisk together remaining coconut milk, peanut butter, soy sauce and garlic chili paste until blended. Set aside.

- Heat sesame oil in skillet on medium-high heat 2 minutes. Add chicken. Cook until browned. Add green onion and bell pepper and cook 10 minutes, covered.

- Add peanut butter mixture and bring to a boil. Cook, stirring constantly, 3 minutes. Serve over rice.

Serves 4

Lettuce Bundles with Spicy Peanut Noodles

2 boneless whole duck or chicken breasts
½ cup plus 3 tablespoons soy sauce, divided
Olive oil
1 large clove garlic
1 (¾-inch) piece ginger, peeled and cut in half
2¼ teaspoons ground fresh chile paste
7 tablespoons smooth, good quality peanut butter
3 tablespoons sugar
4½ tablespoons peanut oil

Juice of 1 lime
4½ tablespoons water
Salt
6 ounces vermicelli or capellini (angel hair) noodles
½ cup roughly chopped, toasted Spanish or other peanuts
2 ounces garlic chives or scallions, cut into 4-inch lengths
1 Japanese or Kirby cucumber, thinly sliced
2 heads Boston or other butterhead lettuce, leaves separated

- Place duck or chicken breasts in a resealable plastic bag along with ½ cup soy sauce, and marinate 1 hour.

- Heat a small amount of olive oil in a grill pan or cast-iron skillet over medium-high heat until very hot. Grill duck or chicken breasts until cooked through, 5 to 7 minutes per side for duck and 4 to 6 minutes per side for chicken. Let cool slightly, and shred with your fingers, or cut into ½-inch wide strips with a knife.

- In a food processor, pulse garlic and ginger until finely chopped. Add chile paste, peanut butter, remaining soy sauce, sugar, peanut oil, lime juice and 4½ tablespoons water, and pulse until smooth. If a thinner sauce is desired, add 1 or 2 more teaspoons water, and pulse to combine. Set aside.

- Bring a large pot of salted water to a boil. Add pasta and cook until al dente, about 8 minutes. Drain in a colander, and rinse with cold water to stop cooking.

- Dress pasta with ½ cup peanut sauce, and transfer to a medium serving bowl. If desired, set the bowl into a larger bowl filled with ice to keep pasta chilled at the table.

- Arrange peanuts, remaining sauce and prepared filling in various serving dishes on the table. Guests can create their own rolls by wrapping noodles, a little sauce, and their choice of meat and fillings in a lettuce leaf.

Serves 6 to 8

Arroz Con Pollo

3	pounds chicken, any combination of pieces	1	(28-ounce) can tomatoes, undrained
½	cup olive oil	1	(4½-ounce) can chopped green chiles
2	cups chopped onion	1	(14½-ounce) can chicken broth
2-3	cloves garlic, crushed	½	cup water
½	teaspoon salt	½	(10-ounce) package frozen peas
½	teaspoon black pepper	½	cup pimiento-stuffed green olives, sliced
2	cups raw converted white rice	1	(4-ounce) jar sliced pimientos, drained
¼	teaspoon saffron threads		

- In a 6-quart Dutch oven or large ovenproof fry pan, heat olive oil and brown chicken until golden brown on all sides. Remove as it browns and set aside.

- Preheat oven to 325°. Add onion, garlic and red pepper to pan. Sauté over medium heat until golden, about 3 minutes. Add salt, pepper, rice and saffron to pan. Cook, stirring for 10 minutes until rice is lightly browned.

- Add tomatoes, green chiles and broth to rice mixture, bring to a boil. Bake 30 minutes, covered. Add chicken and bake, covered, 30 minutes longer.

- Add ½ cup water to pan. Sprinkle peas, olives and pimiento strips over top. Do not stir. Bake, covered, 20 more minutes. Serve hot right from Dutch oven.

Serves 6

Note: If you do not have saffron, use saffron-flavored rice instead.

Scarborough Fair

½ cup plain bread crumbs
2 tablespoons chopped parsley
½ teaspoon sage
½ teaspoon rosemary
½ teaspoon thyme
3 boneless, skinless chicken breasts, split in half
1 stick butter, melted

1 teaspoon salt
1 teaspoon black pepper
8 ounces mozzarella cheese, grated
½ cup all-purpose flour
1 egg, beaten
½ cup dry white wine or sherry

- Preheat oven to 350°.
- Mix bread crumbs, parsley, sage, rosemary and thyme together.
- Pound chicken breasts and brush each with melted butter. Season with salt and pepper and top with grated cheese. Roll chicken and tuck ends under.
- Coat each piece lightly with flour. Dip into beaten egg. Roll chicken in bread crumb mixture.
- Arrange chicken in greased baking dish. Spoon remaining butter over chicken. Bake 20 minutes.
- Add wine and bake 20 more minutes.

Serves 6

Southwest Chicken and Chili Stew

2¼ cups chicken broth

1 pound boneless, skinless chicken breasts, cut into 1-inch cubes

4 cloves garlic

1-2 medium jalapeño peppers, seeded and diced

2 teaspoons all-purpose flour

1 medium red bell pepper, diced

1 medium carrot, sliced (½ cup)

1 (15-ounce) can whole kernel corn, drained

1 (16-ounce) can pinto beans, undrained

2 tablespoons fresh cilantro, finely chopped

½ teaspoon ground cumin

¼ teaspoon salt

¼ teaspoon black pepper

1 teaspoon cornstarch

¼ cup cold water

Tortilla chips

- In a soup kettle, heat ½ cup broth to boiling. Cook chicken in broth for 5 minutes, or until white. Remove chicken from broth with slotted spoon.

- Cook garlic and jalapeños in broth over medium-high heat 2 minutes, stirring frequently. Stir in flour and reduce heat to low. Cook 2 minutes, stirring constantly.

- Gradually stir in remaining broth. Stir in chicken; add bell pepper, carrot, corn, beans, cilantro, cumin, salt and pepper. Heat to boiling. Reduce heat and simmer, covered, 20 minutes, stirring occasionally, until chicken is no longer pink in center.

- Mix cornstarch with cold water and stir into stew. Heat to boiling, stirring frequently.

- Serve with tortilla chips. Chips can be broken into stew on top of individual servings.

Serves 4

Note: Great served with corn muffins.

Pasta with Chicken, Sun-Dried Tomatoes, Gorgonzola and Pine Nuts

½ cup oil-packed sun-dried tomatoes, chopped

2 tablespoons oil from sun-dried tomato jar

2 boneless, skinless chicken breast halves, cut into bite-size pieces

Salt

12-16 ounces medium shell pasta

4 cloves garlic, minced

½ cup chopped fresh basil

½ cup chicken broth

4 ounce package Gorgonzola (blue) cheese, crumbled

¼ cup prosciutto, chopped

Salt and pepper to taste

¼ cup pine nuts, toasted

Reserved pasta water

- Place 6 quarts water in a large pot over high heat.

- Meanwhile, heat 1 tablespoon of sun-dried tomato oil in heavy large skillet over medium-high heat. Add chicken to skillet and sauté until cooked through. Transfer chicken to plate and cool; do not clean skillet.

- When water begins to boil, add 2 tablespoons salt and pasta. Cook pasta until just tender but still firm to bite. Drain pasta; transfer to large bowl.

- Heat remaining tablespoon tomato-oil in same skillet over medium-high heat. Add garlic; sauté until tender about 1 minute. Add sun-dried tomatoes, chicken, basil, broth, cheese and prosciutto to skillet and bring to a boil.

- Add sauce to pasta and toss to coat. Add enough pasta water to adjust consistency. Season with salt and pepper to taste.

- Top with pine nuts and serve.

Serves 4

Bow Ties with Turkey, Pesto and Roasted Red Peppers

1   (12-ounce) package farfalle (bow-tie pasta)
4   cups cubed, cooked turkey or chicken
1   cup basil pesto sauce (see accompanying recipe or use commercial pesto sauce)

1   cup coarsely chopped roasted red bell peppers
1   cup kalamata olives, sliced

• Cook and drain pasta according to package directions. Mix pasta, turkey, pesto, red peppers in saucepan. Heat over low heat, stirring constantly until hot. Garnish with olives.

Variation: Substitute 1 cup chopped sun-dried tomatoes packed in olive oil, drained, for red peppers if desired.

Serves 4

Fresh Cabbage and Sweet Sausage

4   Italian-style sweet sausages or
    4 unseasoned fresh pork sausages
2   potatoes, peeled and quartered

4   cups finely sliced green cabbage
½   cup water

• Place sausages in a skillet and arrange potatoes between them; cover with cabbage and add water. Cover and cook over very low heat. Simmer 1 ½ to 2 hours. This will not burn but will brown.

• Serve with mustard and vinegar.

Serves 2

Basil Pesto Sauce

2 cups packed fresh basil leaves

¾ cup grated Parmesan cheese

½ cup pine nuts, toasted (untoasted walnuts may be substituted)

¾ teaspoon salt

¼ teaspoon black pepper

4 cloves garlic, chopped

¾ cup olive oil

• Place basil, cheese, pine nuts, salt, pepper and garlic into a blender or food processor. Cover and blend on medium speed about 3 minutes, slowly adding olive oil in a steady stream, until smooth.

Note: Basil Pesto Sauce can be frozen.

Southern-Style Bar-B-Q Ribs

2	slabs baby loin back ribs (about 4 pounds)	1	cup Basting Sauce (recipe below)
3	tablespoons Dry Spice Rub (recipe below)	1	cup Sweet Sauce (recipe below)

- Place ribs in a large shallow pan.
- Rub Dry Spice Rub all over ribs. Cover and refrigerate ribs 3 hours prior to cooking.
- Prepare grill. Heat only one side of grill. Place ribs on cool side of grill throughout cooking time. Cook over 300° to 350° coals for 1½ to 2 hours, baste sparingly with Basting Sauce (about every 30 minutes), turning ribs occasionally.
- Brush ribs with Sweet Sauce during last 30 minutes of cooking time.

Dry Spice Rub

3	tablespoons paprika	1	teaspoon red pepper
2	teaspoons seasoned salt	1	teaspoon ground oregano
2	teaspoons black pepper	1	teaspoon dry mustard
2	teaspoons garlic powder	½	teaspoon chili powder

- Combine paprika, seasoned salt, black pepper, garlic powder, red pepper, oregano, mustard and chili powder and mix well.

Basting Sauce

¼	cup firmly packed brown sugar	¼	cup Worcestershire sauce
1½	tablespoons Dry Spice Rub	½	teaspoon hot sauce
2	cups red wine vinegar	1	small bay leaf
2	cups apple juice		

- Combine brown sugar, Dry Spice Rub, vinegar, juice, Worcestershire, hot sauce and bay leaf; cover and let stand at room temperature 8 hours.

Southern-Style Bar-B-Q Ribs continued

Sweet Sauce

1	(8-ounce) can tomato sauce
½	cup spicy honey mustard
1	cup catsup
1	cup red wine vinegar
¼	cup Worcestershire sauce
¼	cup butter
2	tablespoons hot sauce
1	tablespoon lemon juice

2	tablespoons brown sugar
1	tablespoon paprika
1	tablespoon seasoned salt
1½	teaspoons garlic powder
⅛	teaspoon chili powder
⅛	teaspoon red pepper
⅛	teaspoon black pepper

- Combine all ingredients in a Dutch oven. Bring to a boil; reduce heat and simmer 30 minutes, stirring occasionally.

Italian Green Beans

2	pounds fresh green beans
1	pound Italian sausage
2	tablespoons olive oil
3	cloves garlic, minced

	Salt and pepper to taste
	Juice of 1 lemon
1	cup grated Parmesan cheese

- Prepare beans, removing strings and trimming ends. Wash and drain. Place beans in a large pot of salted water and boil until just tender, about 20 minutes. Drain and rinse with cold water to prevent further cooking.

- Fry sausage in a heavy skillet until done and slice into 1-inch pieces. In a clean skillet, add olive oil and garlic; sauté until softened.

- Add beans and sausage and cook until heated through. Add salt and pepper to taste; add lemon juice. When hot, add cheese and serve immediately.

Lake Norman Pork Chops

8	thick pork chops	½	teaspoon thyme
4	tomatoes, thickly sliced	½	teaspoon sage
1	large onion, sliced	2	cups chicken broth
1	bell pepper, coarsely chopped	1	cup white wine
2	(3-ounce) cans mushrooms, drained	1⅓	cups long-grain brown rice, uncooked
	Salt and pepper		

- Preheat oven to 350°.
- In a skillet, brown chops on both sides and place in a buttered 3-quart casserole. Arrange tomatoes, onion, bell peppers and mushrooms on top of chops and season with salt, pepper, thyme and sage.
- In a separate pan, heat broth and wine together.
- Sprinkle raw rice into casserole; pour broth/wine mixture over casserole.
- Cover and bake 45 minutes or until liquid is absorbed and rice is tender.

Serves 6

Honey Mustard and Rosemary Pork

¾   cup beer
½   cup Dijon mustard
6   tablespoons honey
¼   cup olive oil

2   tablespoons chopped garlic
2   tablespoons fresh or 1 tablespoon dried rosemary
1   (1- to 2-pound) boneless pork loin roast
½   cup whipping cream

- Whisk beer, mustard, honey, olive oil, garlic and rosemary together. Pour into an 8 x 8 x 2-inch square pan or a resealable plastic bag large enough to hold roast. Let stand at room temperature at least one hour. (If marinating longer, refrigerate; remove 1 hour before cooking.)

- Preheat oven to 350°.

- Transfer pork to rack and set in roasting pan. Reserve marinade. Roast until meat thermometer reaches 150°, about 55 minutes. Remove from oven and let rest 15 minutes while preparing sauce.

- Strain reserved marinade into large heavy skillet. Add cream and any juices from roasting pan. Do not add any burned bits from roasting pan. Bring to a boil; reduce heat to medium and simmer at least 15 minutes.

- Slice pork and serve with sauce on the side.

Serves 4

Pork with Carolina Peaches

Jezebel Sauce

1 cup apple jelly

1 cup pineapple-orange marmalade or pineapple preserves

1 (6-ounce) jar prepared mustard

1 (4-ounce) jar prepared horseradish

¼ teaspoon black pepper

• In a mixing bowl, beat apple jelly with an electric mixer at medium speed until smooth.

• Add marmalade, mustard, horseradish and pepper; beat at medium speed until blended. Chill.

Makes 3 cups

1	(3½-pound) boneless pork loin roast	Salt and pepper to taste
1	bunch fresh thyme, leaves picked, divided	15 slices pancetta or bacon
1	whole bulb garlic, peeled, divided	¾ cup white wine, divided
1¾	sticks butter	1 tablespoon all-purpose flour
2	(15-ounce) cans peaches in natural juice, drained, divided	¾ cup water

• Preheat oven to 425°.

• If you can find a loin with the fat still on the back, it will keep the meat very moist and tender. Score skin of pork through the fat. Turn over. Make a pocket in the meat by slicing at an angle towards the center of loin. Do not cut all the way through meat.

• Chop half the thyme with 1 clove garlic and mix together with butter, 1 can of peaches and a good pinch of salt and pepper. Push butter into the pocket and pat back into shape. Lay pancetta over the pork, leaving skin side uncovered. Tie firmly with 3 to 4 pieces of kitchen string.

• Place loin, skin side up, in a roasting pan with remaining peaches, garlic cloves, thyme and half the wine. Roast about 1 hour until skin is crisp and golden.

• When ready, remove pork and peaches to a plate and allow to rest 15 minutes while preparing sauce. Remove most of fat from roasting pan and place pan over high heat. Mash cooked garlic and add to pan with flour. Stir and add remaining wine; add water. Simmer a few minutes until reduced. Strain and add any extra juices from rested pork. Check seasoning of sauce and drizzle over sliced pork.

Serves 6 to 8

Slow Cooker Teriyaki Pork Loin

¾ cup apple juice
2 tablespoons sugar
2 tablespoons soy sauce
1 tablespoon vinegar
1 teaspoon ground ginger

¼ teaspoon garlic powder
⅛ teaspoon black pepper
1 (2- to 3-pound) lean boneless rolled pork loin roast
3 tablespoons cold water
1½ tablespoons cornstarch

- In slow cooker, mix apple juice, sugar, soy sauce, vinegar, ginger, garlic powder and pepper. Add roast, turning to coat. Turn fat side up.

- Cover and cook on high for 3½ to 4 hours or on low for 7 to 8 hours or until meat is very tender.

- Transfer meat to warm platter. Cover and keep warm.

- Strain cooking liquid and place in a small saucepan; you should have about 1⅔ cup liquid. Skim off fat if desired. Bring to a boil over medium heat.

- Meanwhile in a small bowl, mix water and cornstarch until smooth. Stir cornstarch mixture into boiling liquid and boil 1 to 2 minutes or until sauce has thickened. Serve sauce separately.

Note: Great with fried rice and stir-fried Oriental vegetables.

Pork Tenderloin Towers

8	slices bacon		**Salt and pepper**
4	slices onion	4	(½-inch) tomato slices
1	(¾-pound) pork tenderloin, cut into 4 (1-inch) slices	4	slices Swiss cheese

- Prepare gas or charcoal grill.
- Layer 2 slices bacon to form an X. Place one slice onion in center of bacon and top with one slice tenderloin. Sprinkle with salt and pepper. Bring ends of bacon over tenderloin and secure with a wooden pick. Repeat procedure with remaining bacon, onion and tenderloin.
- Place meat on grill over medium coals, and grill 40 minutes turning frequently. Turn meat with wooden pick side up and remove wooden picks. Top each with a slice of tomato and cheese; then grill 10 additional minutes.

Serves 4

Sausage Bowties

12 ounces uncooked farfalle (bowtie pasta)
    Olive oil
1   pound sweet or hot Italian sausage, casing removed,
      crumbled
½   teaspoon crushed red pepper
½   cup finely chopped onion
3   cloves garlic, crushed or minced

1   (28-ounce) can chopped tomatoes, drained
1½ cups heavy cream
½   teaspoon salt
2   teaspoons pesto (optional)
    Salt and pepper to taste
3   tablespoons finely chopped fresh parsley
¾-1 cup grated Parmesan cheese

- Cook pasta in boiling water until al dente.

- Meanwhile, heat a small amount of oil in a heavy skillet over medium heat. Add sausage and red pepper. Sauté for 7 minutes or until sausage is no longer pink. Add onion and garlic and sauté until onion is tender and sausage is lightly browned.

- Stir in tomatoes, cream and pesto. Season with salt and pepper. Simmer 4 minutes or until mixture is slightly thickened and flavors have blended.

- Drain pasta and add to sausage mixture in skillet. Cook 2 minutes, stirring occasionally. Add parsley and Parmesan cheese. Toss to mix well.

Serves 6 to 8

Grandfather Mountain Brisket

Versatile Meat Marinade

½ cup olive oil

½ cup soy sauce

½ cup pineapple or orange juice

1 clove garlic, minced

½ teaspoon coarsely ground black pepper

Chicken breasts, pork, lamb chops, or steaks

• Whisk oil, soy sauce, juice, garlic and pepper together in a bowl. Pour into a large resealable plastic bag. Add meat of choice and refrigerate 4 to 6 hours.

Makes 1½ cups

1	(3-pound) brisket	⅓	cup barbecue sauce
	Garlic salt	2	teaspoons soy sauce
	Seasoned salt	½	cup red or port wine
1	large onion, sliced	2	teaspoons brown sugar

• Preheat oven to 350°.

• Place brisket in a 13 x 9 x 2-inch pan and sprinkle with garlic salt and seasoned salt until heavily covered.

• Arrange onion over meat.

• Combine barbecue sauce, soy sauce, wine and brown sugar until well blended. Pour over roast and cover tightly with foil.

• Bake 3 hours.

• Remove meat from pan and reserve pan drippings. Cool slightly and slice meat. Serve with Sauce.

Sauce

1	(14-ounce) can sliced mushrooms, drained, reserving liquid	2	tablespoons all-purpose flour

• Dissolve flour in mushroom liquid. Add flour mixture and mushrooms to pan drippings. Cook until sauce has thickened. Pour sauce over sliced meat.

Beef Wellingtons with Gorgonzola

4	(6-ounce) center-cut filet mignons, 1½-inch thick	1	tablespoon minced garlic
	Salt and pepper	1	large egg
4	large mushrooms (about ¼ pound total), thinly sliced		All-purpose flour for dusting
1	tablespoon unsalted butter	1	sheet frozen puff pastry, thawed
1	tablespoon finely chopped shallot	4	tablespoons Gorgonzola cheese (about 2½ ounces)

- Preheat oven to 425°.

- Pat filet mignons dry and season with salt and pepper. In a shallow roasting pan, roast filets in middle of oven 12 minutes, or until a meat thermometer registers 110° for rare; and cool (filets will be baked again after being wrapped in pastry). Chill filets, covered, until cold, about 1 hour.

- In a heavy skillet, combine mushrooms with butter, shallots, garlic, salt and pepper to taste. Cook over moderate heat, stirring, until mushrooms are lightly browned. Transfer mushroom mixture to a bowl to cool completely.

- In a small bowl, lightly beat egg to make an egg wash.

- On a lightly floured surface, roll out puff pastry sheet into a 14-inch square. Trim edges to form a 13-inch square and cut into 4 (6½-inch) squares.

- Put 1 tablespoon Gorgonzola in center of each square and top with ¼ mushroom mixture. Top mushroom mixture with a filet, pressing it down gently, and wrap 2 opposite corners of puff pastry over filet, overlapping them. Seal seam with egg wash. Wrap remaining 2 corners of pastry over filet to enclose completely. Repeat procedure for 3 remaining filets.

- Arrange Beef Wellingtons, seam side down, in a nonstick baking pan. Chill Beef Wellingtons, loosely covered, at least 1 hour or up to 1 day. Chill remaining egg wash for brushing on pastry just before baking.

- When ready to cook, preheat oven to 425°.

- Brush top and sides of each Beef Wellington with remaining egg wash and bake 20 minutes, or until pastry is golden.

- While Beef Wellingtons are baking, make sauce.

Sauce

1	cup veal or beef demi-glace	2	tablespoons Madeira wine

- In a saucepan, stir demi-glace and Madeira together and boil 1 minute. Keep sauce warm until ready to serve. Serve with Beef Wellingtons.

Tournedos Diables

1	(4-pound) beef tenderloin	1	tablespoon tomato paste
	Coarsely ground black pepper	1	tablespoon Worcestershire sauce
	Garlic salt	1	tablespoon white vinegar
12	slices bacon	½	teaspoon garlic powder
1	cup beef broth diluted with 1 cup water	¼	teaspoon cayenne pepper
¼	cup cognac	1	cup sliced fresh mushrooms
¼	cup sherry	2	shallots, chopped
2	tablespoons Dijon mustard	2	green onions, chopped
1	tablespoon butter or margarine	6	cups hot cooked rice

- Trim fat from beef. Slice into 12 (1-inch thick) slices. Rub both sides of each slice with pepper and garlic salt. Wrap 1 slice bacon around edge of each slice beef; secure with wooden picks.

- Prepare gas or charcoal grill.

- Bring broth to a boil in a heavy saucepan; reduce heat, and simmer 3 minutes. Heat cognac and sherry in a small saucepan just until hot (do not boil); remove from heat, ignite with a long match, and pour over broth. When flame dies down, add mustard, butter or margarine, tomato paste, Worcestershire sauce, vinegar, garlic powder and cayenne. Cook over low heat 15 minutes. Stir in mushrooms, green onions and shallots. Cover and simmer 5 minutes.

- Grill bacon-wrapped tenderloin slices, covered with grill lid, over medium coals (300°-350°) 10 minutes on each side or to desired degree of doneness. Remove wooden picks. Arrange tenderloin slices over rice on platter; spoon mushroom sauce over meat.

Serves 12

Old English Prime Rib

---

1 boneless rib eye roast
2 boxes kosher salt
¼ cup Worcestershire sauce

Freshly ground black pepper to taste
Water

- Preheat oven to 375°-400°.

- Pour 1 entire box of kosher salt in bottom of a roasting pan. Place rib eye roast on top of salt. Dust liberally with freshly ground black pepper and pour Worcestershire over top.

- Pour remaining box of kosher salt over top of rib eye, taking care to coat completely. Sprinkle with water.

- Bake approximately 2 hours, using a meat thermometer to check doneness. The kosher salt will form a hard shell around the roast, sealing in juices. When done, crack the shell open with a hammer and enjoy!

Note: End pieces of roast will be well done and much saltier. The roast will be rare toward the center.

Horseradish Mousse

1 envelope unflavored gelatin	1 cup sour cream
½ cup water	½ teaspoon salt
¾ cup prepared horseradish	2 tablespoons green peppercorns, drained, lightly crushed
1 teaspoon Dijon mustard	2 tablespoons very finely chopped green onion tops for garnish
1 cup heavy cream	

- Stir gelatin into water and allow to stand until softened, 5 minutes.

- Drain horseradish thoroughly and squeeze dry in towel.

- Blend together mustard and cream in medium saucepan. Bring to simmer over medium heat. Remove from heat and whisk in softened gelatin.

- In separate bowl, gradually whisk mustard mixture into sour cream until well incorporated. Stir in horseradish, salt and peppercorns.

- Pour mousse mixture into oiled 4-cup mold or soufflé dish. Cover loosely with plastic wrap and refrigerate 6 hours or until set, but not more than 1 day.

- Unmold onto serving plate and sprinkle with chopped green onion tops.

Cardamom Eye of Round Roast

4-5	pound eye of round	½	teaspoon garlic powder
¼	cup coarsely ground black pepper	1	teaspoon paprika
½	tablespoon ground cardamom	1	cup soy sauce
1	can tomato paste	¾	cup vinegar

- Mix pepper and cardamom together. Cover roast and press mixture in.

- In a shallow baking dish, mix tomato paste, garlic powder and paprika. Gradually add soy sauce and vinegar. Add beef to dish and marinate for 24 to 48 hours in refrigerator. Turn occasionally.

- When ready to cook, preheat oven to 350°.

- Remove beef and wrap in foil with some of the marinade. Bake 2 hours. Slice and serve warm or cold with Horseradish Mousse or Red Wine Sauce.

Note: Perfect for main dish; also, great served cold, sliced for parties.

Red Wine Sauce For Beef

⅓ cup Worcestershire sauce

⅓ cup catsup

2 tablespoons brown sugar

⅔ cup red wine

1 teaspoon dry mustard

1 (4-ounce) can sliced mushrooms, drained

5 tablespoons melted butter

- Blend all ingredients and serve warm as accompaniment for roasted beef or steak.

Marinated Flank Steak

Orange-Balsamic Marinade

⅓ cup Grand Marnier

3 tablespoons balsamic vinegar

3 tablespoons Worcestershire

1 tablespoon extra-virgin olive oil

3 cloves garlic, crushed

• Mix Grand Marnier, vinegar, Worcestershire, olive oil and garlic.

• Marinate flank steak overnight.

Flank steak
Meat tenderizer
¼ cup soy sauce
½ cup oil
¼-⅓ cup Worcestershire sauce

1 generous tablespoon honey
½ teaspoon ginger
½ teaspoon garlic powder
1 tablespoon minced onion

• Score steak and sprinkle with tenderizer. Mix additional tenderizer with soy sauce, oil, Worcestershire, honey, ginger, garlic powder and onion and pour over steak. Marinate several hours or overnight.

• Grill over charcoal coals 10 to 12 minutes on each side.

Serves 4 to 6

Note: This marinade is also good on chicken or London broil.

Sauerbraten

5-6 pound round or rump roast

Vinegar Marinade

2 cups red wine vinegar
4 cups water
1 cup thinly sliced onion
4-5 peppercorns
1 bay leaf

¼ teaspoon thyme
2 cloves
1 pinch ground nutmeg
   Several parsley sprigs

Sauce

¼ cup all-purpose flour
2 tablespoons butter
2 carrots, sliced
1-2 onions, quartered
1 tablespoon catsup
½-⅔ cup crushed gingersnaps

2 tablespoons sugar
1 teaspoon browning-and-seasoning sauce
½ cup red wine
½ cup raisins
½ cup slivered almonds

- Place beef in large, deep bowl. Prepare marinade in a saucepan by combining red wine vinegar, water, onion, peppercorns, bay leaf, thyme, cloves, nutmeg and parsley. Bring to a boil and pour over meat. Marinate in refrigerator 3 days, turning several times.

- Remove meat from marinade. Reserve liquid and strain. Wipe meat dry, dredge with flour and sauté in butter in a large, heavy Dutch oven until well browned. Add carrots, onion, catsup and 1 cup of reserved marinade. Refrigerate remaining marinade.

- Cover and simmer 3 hours until tender. Remove roast to heated platter; keep warm.

- Strain sauce from Dutch oven, skim off fat; measure liquid to make 2 cups. If not enough, add enough marinade to make 2 cups. Add gingersnaps, sugar, browning-and-seasoning sauce, wine and raisins to broth and boil until sauce has thickened. Add almonds and cook a few minutes longer.

- Slice meat and serve with sauce.

Sunday Afternoon Beef Brisket

1   (4-pound) beef brisket

Rub Mix

2   tablespoons chili powder
2   tablespoons salt
1   tablespoon garlic powder
1   tablespoon onion powder
1   tablespoon black pepper

1   tablespoon sugar
2   teaspoons dry mustard
1   bay leaf, crushed
    Beef stock or beef broth

- Preheat oven to 350°.
- Mix together chili powder, salt, garlic powder, onion powder, pepper, sugar, mustard and bay leaf. Season brisket on both sides with rub.
- Place in roasting pan, uncovered. Cover for 1 hour. Add beef stock or beef broth to yield ½-inch of liquid in bottom of pan. Reduce heat to 300°.
- Cover and continue cooking 3 hours, or longer.
- Slice meat across the grain, top with juice from pan.

Hot Reuben Casserole

2   (10-ounce) cans chopped sauerkraut, drained
1   pound thinly sliced corned beef, coarsely chopped
¾   cup Thousand Island dressing

8   ounces thinly sliced Swiss cheese
5½ cups (about 8 ounces) coarsely crumbled rye bread
¼   cup butter or margarine, melted

- Preheat oven to 375°.
- In a greased 11 x 7 x 2-inch baking dish, layer sauerkraut, corned beef, dressing, cheese and rye bread and drizzle with butter.
- Bake, uncovered, 30 to 40 minutes or until casserole is heated through and bread crumbs are lightly browned.

Serves 6 to 8

Beef Stew with Tomatoes

3 tablespoons olive oil

1½ pounds beef bottom round or boneless short ribs

1 large onion, cut in half and then into ½-inch thick slices

1 (28-ounce) can whole tomatoes in purée with juices

2 tablespoons red wine vinegar

2 tablespoons brown sugar

½ teaspoon ground ginger

1 teaspoon ground cinnamon

1 bay leaf

4 large carrots, peeled and cut into 1-inch pieces

4 white boiling potatoes, peeled and cut into 1-inch cubes (Yukon gold are great; even better with 2 sweet potatoes instead)

Salt and pepper

- In an 8-quart heavy-bottomed stew pot over medium-high heat, warm olive oil. Add beef and brown well on all sides, about 5 minutes. Add onion and sauté, stirring, until softened, 2 to 3 minutes. Add tomatoes and juices, vinegar, brown sugar, ginger, cinnamon and bay leaf; stir well. Bring to a simmer, reduce heat to medium low, cover and simmer gently for 30 minutes.

- Add carrots and potatoes; continue to gently simmer until meat and vegetables are tender, about one hour longer. Discard bay leaf and season to taste with salt and pepper.

- To serve, transfer meat to a cutting board and cut across the grain into thick slices. Place slices in warmed bowls and spoon vegetable mixture over top.

Serves 4

Marion Street Meat Loaf

Hot Dog Chili

2 pounds ground beef,
browned and drained

½ (18-ounce) bottle
barbecue sauce

½ cup catsup

2 teaspoons chili
powder

1 teaspoon sugar

2-3 dashes soy sauce

2-3 dashes
Worcestershire sauce

1 dash garlic powder

2 dashes hot sauce

1 dash red pepper

Salt and pepper
to taste

• Combine beef,
barbecue sauce, catsup,
chili powder, sugar, soy
sauce, Worcestershire,
garlic powder, hot sauce,
red pepper, salt and
pepper.

• Simmer 2 hours. Serve
with hot dogs.

Makes approximately 3 cups

*Note: Also good as a dip for
nacho chips. May be frozen.*

3	tablespoons butter	¼	teaspoon ground white pepper
¾	cup finely chopped onion	¼	teaspoon cayenne pepper
¾	cup finely chopped scallions, white bulb and 3 inches of green	1	teaspoon ground cumin
½	cup finely chopped carrots	½	teaspoon freshly grated nutmeg
¼	cup finely chopped celery	3	eggs, well beaten
¼	cup minced red bell pepper	½	cup catsup
¼	cup minced green bell pepper	½	cup half & half
2	teaspoons minced garlic	2	pounds lean ground beef chuck
	Salt to taste	12	ounces bulk sausage, not fennel-flavored Italian sausage
1	teaspoon freshly ground black pepper	¾	cup fine fresh bread crumbs, toasted

- Preheat oven to 375°.

- Melt butter in a heavy skillet; add onion, scallions, carrots, celery, bell peppers and garlic. Cook, stirring often, until moisture from vegetables has evaporated, about 10 minutes. Set aside to cool.

- Combine salt, black pepper, cayenne, cumin, nutmeg and eggs in a mixing bowl; beat well. Add catsup and half & half. Blend thoroughly.

- Add beef, sausage and bread crumbs to egg mixture. Add cooled vegetables and mix thoroughly by hand, kneading 5 minutes.

- With damp hands, form mixture into an oval approximately 17 x 4½ x 1½-inches, resembling a long loaf of bread.

- Place meat loaf in a baking dish. Bake in oven for 35 to 40 minutes.

- Let rest 20 minutes before slicing and serving.

Serves 8 to 10

Veal Scaloppine Marsala

8	scaloppine of veal (veal cutlets pounded thin)	2	tablespoons finely chopped shallots, divided
	Salt and pepper to taste	2	cups shiitake or cremino mushrooms
	All-purpose flour	½	cup dry Marsala wine
⅓	cup vegetable oil	½	cup chicken stock
1	stick butter, divided	2	tablespoons parsley, chopped

- Lightly salt and pepper veal, dredge in flour and shake off excess. In a wide skillet, heat vegetable oil until hot, but not smoking. Sauté floured veal on both sides until golden and set on a plate. Drain oil and return to heat. Add half of the butter and shallots. Cook a few minutes until wilted, add mushrooms, salt and pepper; sauté over medium heat until all water has evaporated from mushrooms, about 10 minutes. Add Marsala wine and continue to cook until all alcohol has evaporated, about 7 minutes. Add remaining butter and chicken stock, bring all to a vigorous boil and season with salt and pepper. When reduced by half, add meat and let simmer 5 minutes. Add parsley and serve. Delicious with rice.

Note: Thinly sliced boneless, skinless chicken breasts may be substituted for veal.

Grilled Leg of Lamb

2	pints plain regular or low fat yogurt	¾	cup fresh whole rosemary leaves (2 large bunches)
½	cup olive oil, plus more for brushing grill	2	teaspoons kosher salt
	Zest of 1 lemon	1	teaspoon freshly ground black pepper
	Juice of 3 lemons (about ½ cup)	1	(5-pound) leg of lamb, butterflied (9 pounds if bone-in)

- Combine yogurt, olive oil, lemon zest and juice, rosemary, salt and pepper in a large non-reactive bowl. Add lamb, making sure to completely cover with marinade. Marinate in refrigerator, covered, overnight or up to 3 days.

- Bring lamb to room temperature. Prepare charcoal grill with hot coals or gas grill. Scrape marinade off lamb, wipe meat with paper towels; season generously with salt and pepper.

- Brush grill with olive oil to prevent lamb from sticking. Grill lamb on both sides until internal temperature is 120°-125° for rare, 40 minutes to 1 hour, depending on how hot grill is.

- Remove lamb to a cutting board, cover with foil and allow to rest 20 minutes. Slice and serve.

Serves 8 to 12

Continental-Style Leg of Lamb

Leg of lamb, boned, at room temperature
3-4 cloves garlic to taste
Salt and pepper to taste
½ teaspoon marjoram
½ teaspoon thyme

½ teaspoon rosemary
2 tablespoons tomato paste
¼ cup dry white wine (Vermouth)
1 cup stock or water, plus more for gravy
Cornstarch

- Preheat oven to 325°.

- Slice garlic, reserving one clove. Make several incisions in meat and insert small slivers of garlic. Rub entire surface of lamb with one cut clove garlic. Sprinkle well with salt, pepper, marjoram, thyme and rosemary.

- Combine tomato paste with wine and 1 cup stock or water. Place meat on trivet in a shallow roasting pan with fat side up. Pour liquids over meat and roast until done. Baste every 15 minutes with drippings in pan, adding more stock or water as needed, to prevent scorching. Turn meat once about half way through roasting time.

- Test doneness with an instant-read thermometer in thickest part of leg (140°-145° for medium rare, 160° for medium or 170° for well done). When lamb is done, remove and place on warm platter.

- Prepare gravy by adding enough stock or water to drippings in roasting pan to make amount of gravy desired. For each cup, add 1 tablespoon cornstarch (or 2 tablespoons flour) combined with 2 or 3 tablespoons water to make smooth paste. Combine with drippings and cook, stirring continuously until thickened, then simmer about 5 minutes. Taste and season further, if necessary.

- Slice thinly with the grain of the meat.

Serves 6-8

Note: Allow 45 minutes cooking time per pound for roasting.

Mushroom Quiche

1   (9-inch) pie shell
1   small onion, chopped
½   pound fresh mushrooms, sliced
2   tablespoons olive oil
3   eggs, beaten
½   cup evaporated milk

1   (8-ounce) carton sour cream
½   teaspoon ground nutmeg
1   teaspoon salt
½   teaspoon black pepper
½   pound Swiss cheese, diced
1   tablespoon all-purpose flour

- Preheat oven to 425°.
- Prick pastry shell with fork. Bake 6 to 8 minutes. Let cool. Reduce oven temperature to 350°.
- Sauté onion and mushrooms in olive oil until tender. Drain excess oil.
- In a large bowl, combine eggs, milk, sour cream, nutmeg, salt and pepper.
- In a separate bowl, combine cheese and flour; add to egg mixture. Stir in onion and mushrooms.
- Pour into pastry shell and bake 45 minutes or until set.

Asparagus Quiche

1   (9-inch) pie shell
8   slices bacon, crisply cooked
2   cups fresh asparagus cut into 1-inch pieces and
      steamed
1   cup shredded Gruyère or Swiss cheese
1   cup light cream or half & half

3   eggs, slightly beaten
1   teaspoon dried tarragon or 1 tablespoon minced fresh
¼   teaspoon nutmeg
½   teaspoon salt
    Dash black pepper

- Preheat oven to 450°.
- Prick pastry shell with fork and bake 7 minutes; cool. Reduce oven temperature to 350°.
- Crumble bacon into shell. Add asparagus, then cheese.
- In a bowl, mix cream, eggs, tarragon, nutmeg, salt and pepper. Pour gently over cheese.
- Bake 30 minutes or until set and puffy.

Spinach Tart

Pastry for Double Crust Pie

2   cups all-purpose flour
½   teaspoon salt
⅔   cup shortening

5-6 tablespoons plus 1 tablespoon cold water
1   tablespoon fresh basil or oregano
1   egg

- Combine flour and salt. Cut in shortening. Sprinkle with 1 tablespoon cold water. Repeat until dough is moistened, reserving 1 tablespoon cold water for egg wash. Add fresh herbs. Divide into 2 equal sections.

- Roll dough to form a 10-inch circle. Place in a tart pan, if available. If not, free-form crust on a cookie sheet and scallop edges with back of a knife.

Spinach Filling

1   (10-ounce) bag fresh spinach, torn into pieces
1   (8-ounce) package cream cheese, softened
¼   cup sour cream
2-4 cloves garlic, minced

¼   teaspoon salt
¼   teaspoon black pepper
½   cup chopped water chestnuts

- Reduce oven temperature to 425°

- In a saucepan with water, cook spinach 2 to 4 minutes; drain and press through a colander.

- In a bowl, combine cream cheese, sour cream, garlic, salt, pepper and water chestnuts. Add spinach.

- Spread spinach filling over pastry leaving ½-inch margin on all sides. Moisten edge with water.

- Top with second pastry round. Seal and flute edges. Cut a slit in top of dough to release steam.

- Combine reserved tablespoon water and egg. Brush pastry with egg wash.

- Bake 20 to 25 minutes.

Green and White Lasagna

9	lasagna noodles, cooked		2	cups milk
½	cup chopped onion		1	(10-ounce) frozen chopped spinach, thawed and drained
2	tablespoons butter			
2	tablespoons cornstarch		1	(3.8-ounce) can sliced black olives
1	tablespoon parsley		1¾	cups ricotta cheese
1	teaspoon dried basil		1	egg, beaten
¼	teaspoon garlic powder		2	cups shredded mozzarella cheese
⅛	teaspoon ground nutmeg		½	cup grated Parmesan cheese, divided

- Preheat oven to 350°.

- Sauté onion in butter until tender. Stir in cornstarch, parsley, basil, garlic powder and nutmeg. Add milk. Cook and stir until thickened. Add spinach and olives; set aside.

- Combine ricotta cheese and egg. Add mozzarella cheese and ½ of the Parmesan cheese; set aside.

- Arrange 3 lasagna noodles on bottom of a 13 x 9 x 2-inch baking dish. Top with ⅓ of spinach mixture, then ⅓ ricotta cheese mixture. Repeat twice. Top with remaining Parmesan cheese.

- Bake, covered with foil, 55 minutes. Uncover and cook 5 more minutes.

Note: May be frozen.

Fettuccine Alfredo

1	stick butter		½	pint heavy cream
2	cloves garlic, crushed		12	ounces fettuccine, cooked
¾	cup ricotta cheese			Salt and pepper to taste
½	cup Parmesan cheese			Chopped parsley

- Melt butter, then add garlic, ricotta cheese, Parmesan cheese and cream. Simmer over low heat until thickened.

- Meanwhile, boil fettuccine noodles to desired doneness and drain thoroughly. Pour cream mixture over drained hot noodles. Sprinkle parsley on top.

- To reheat, add heavy cream or half & half.

Ratatouille with Penne

Marinara Sauce

½ cup olive oil

4-6 cloves garlic, crushed

2 (28-ounce) cans crushed tomatoes in purée

2 tablespoons dried basil or 3 leaves fresh basil, chopped

Salt and pepper to taste

• In a large pot, sauté garlic on medium-low heat for about 1 minutes. Add tomatoes, basil, salt and pepper. Stir frequently, making sure to stir to bottom of the pot. Simmer on low 30 to 40 minutes.

2 eggplants (1½ pounds), cut into ½-inch cubes

4 onions, chopped

½ cup olive oil, divided
kosher salt to taste

4 yellow squash (1½ pounds), cut into ½-inch cubes

2 large red bell peppers, cut into ½-inch cubes

8 plum tomatoes, peeled, seeded and chopped

7 cloves garlic, minced

1 teaspoon chopped fresh thyme

1½ pounds penne rigate (penne pasta with ridges)

½ cup finely chopped fresh flat-leaf parsley

¼ cup finely chopped fresh basil
Grated Parmiagiano-Reggiano cheese

• Preheat oven to 450°.

• In a large roasting pan, stir together eggplant, onion, ¼ cup olive oil and kosher salt. Roast mixture in middle of oven, stirring occasionally, 15 minutes. Stir in squash, bell peppers, 2 tablespoons olive oil and more kosher salt and roast mixture, stirring occasionally, until bell peppers are tender, about 25 to 30 minutes.

• While vegetables are roasting, simmer tomatoes, garlic, thyme, remaining 2 tablespoons olive oil and kosher salt in a heavy saucepan, stirring occasionally, 12 to 15 minutes or until thickened. Stir tomatoes into roasted vegetables and season with salt and pepper to taste.

• Cook penne in a pot of boiling, salted water until al dente and drain.

• While pasta is cooking, stir parsley and basil into ratatouille and season. Toss pasta with ⅓ of ratatouille and top with remainder. Top with grated Parmesan cheese.

Serves 6

Note: Ratatouille may be made 2 days ahead and chilled, covered. Reheat before adding to pasta. For a quick dish, use a jar of prepared sauce rather than homemade Marinara Sauce.

Macaroni with Three Cheeses

12	ounces dry macaroni	¼	teaspoon nutmeg
½	cup chopped bell pepper	2	cups milk
⅓	cup plus 1 tablespoon butter, divided	1	cup shredded provolone cheese
⅓	cup all-purpose flour	1	cup shredded Cheddar cheese
¼	teaspoon salt	½-¾	cup crumbled blue cheese
¼	teaspoon black pepper	¼	cup seasoned dry bread crumbs

- Preheat oven to 350°.
- Boil macaroni according to package directions; rinse and drain.
- In a saucepan, sauté bell pepper in ½ cup of butter about 5 minutes. Add flour, salt, pepper and nutmeg. Gradually add milk. Cook until thickened. Remove from heat.
- Add provolone cheese, Cheddar cheese and blue cheese; stir until melted. Stir in macaroni. Place in 13 x 9 x 2-inch baking dish.
- Melt 1 tablespoon butter and add bread crumbs; sprinkle over macaroni.
- Bake 30 minutes.

Serves 6

Homecoming Macaroni and Cheese

1	(8-ounce) package macaroni	12	ounces cream-style cottage cheese
1	egg	1	(8-ounce) carton sour cream
1	cup milk	1	pound regular or sharp Cheddar cheese, grated, divided
¾	teaspoon salt		Paprika

- Preheat oven to 350°.
- Boil macaroni according to package directions and drain.
- Slightly beat egg. Add milk and salt. Add cottage cheese, sour cream and all but ½ cup cheese. Add macaroni and mix.
- Place in greased 3-quart casserole dish. Sprinkle with remaining cheese and paprika. Bake 45 minutes.

Serves 4

Baked Manicotti with Salsa di Pomadori

Salsa di Pomadori

¼ cup olive oil
1 cup finely chopped onion
1 clove garlic, crushed
1 (6-ounce) can tomato paste
2 teaspoons dried parsley
1 teaspoon salt

3 (14.5-ounce) cans Italian-style tomatoes, undrained
2 teaspoons sugar
1 tablespoon oregano
1 teaspoon dried basil
¼ teaspoon black pepper
1½ cups water

- Heat olive oil in a Dutch oven. Sauté onion until transparent.
- Add garlic, stirring constantly to prevent burning. Add tomato paste, parsley, salt, tomatoes, sugar, oregano, basil, pepper and water. Mix well, mashing tomatoes with a fork.
- Bring to a boil, reduce heat and simmer 1 hour, stirring occasionally.

Manicotti Filling

1 (8-ounce) box manicotti shells
2 tablespoons olive oil
1 pound ground round beef
1 clove garlic, crushed
½ cup chopped onion
1 teaspoon dried oregano
1 teaspoon salt

¼ teaspoon black pepper
1 cup cottage cheese
8 ounces grated mozzarella cheese
½ cup mayonnaise
⅔ cup grated Parmesan cheese, divided
2 eggs, beaten
1 tablespoon chopped parsley

- Preheat oven to 350°.
- Boil manicotti shells according to package instructions; drain and set aside.
- In a large saucepan, brown beef, garlic and onion in olive oil. Drain fat. Add oregano, salt and pepper.
- In a large mixing bowl, combine cottage cheese, mozzarella, mayonnaise, ⅓ cup Parmesan cheese, eggs and parsley. Blend mixture well. Add meat and stir.
- Stuff each shell with cheese-meat mixture. Spread a thin layer of salsa in bottom of a 13 x 9 x 2-inch baking dish. Place shells in a single layer. Top with remaining salsa.
- Sprinkle with a thin layer of remaining Parmesan cheese. Bake, uncovered, 30 minutes or until bubbling.

Serves 8

Pasta with Tomato and Four Cheeses

2¾ pounds tomatoes, cored, seeded and diced
½ cup fresh basil, shredded
1½ teaspoons kosher salt
1 large clove garlic, minced
1 cup ricotta cheese, room temperature
2 tablespoons whipping cream
Dash black pepper

Dash nutmeg
2 ounces fontina cheese, diced
2 ounces mozzarella cheese, diced
1 pound rotelle pasta
2 tablespoons olive oil
1 cup grated Parmesan cheese

- Combine tomatoes, basil, salt and garlic and let stand 1 to 2 hours, stirring occasionally.

- Fluff ricotta with a fork. Add whipping cream, pepper and nutmeg and blend until creamy. Add fontina cheese and mozzarella cheese; mix well.

- Drain most of liquid from tomatoes, leaving just enough to keep moist.

- In a large pot, boil pasta according to package directions. Drain and place pasta in a large heated serving bowl and toss with olive oil. Add cheese mixture and toss until cheese begins to melt. Spoon tomato mixture over top and garnish with more Parmesan cheese.

Serves 6

Angel Hair Pasta with Asparagus, Tomatoes and Basil

16	spears fresh asparagus		¼	teaspoon black pepper
1	tablespoon olive oil		1	tablespoon butter, do not substitute
4	cloves garlic, finely chopped		9	ounces angel hair pasta, cooked
6	Roma tomatoes, chopped		¼	cup fresh chopped basil
¼	cup dry white wine			Grated Parmesan cheese (optional)
¼	teaspoon salt			

- Cut asparagus spears into 1½-inch pieces, setting asparagus tips aside.

- Heat oil over medium heat. Add garlic, stirring constantly. Add tomatoes and cook 2 minutes.

- Add asparagus spears, wine, salt and pepper. Cook, uncovered, 3 minutes. Add asparagus tips and cook 1 more minute. Add butter and stir until melted.

- Stir in cooked, drained pasta. Add basil. Top with grated Parmesan cheese, if desired. Serve immediately.

Serves 4 to 6

Side Dishes

Cedar Rock Falls

Journey along the Cedar Creek in the Pisgah National Forest and before long you'll hear the gentle rush of water flowing over Cedar Rock Falls. When you reach the falls you'll find a luxuriant carpet of moss-covered rocks strewn about the pool. The fragrant aroma of rhododendron fills the air. It is a cool and shady locale that provides a respite even on the hottest summer day. Whether a Saturday afternoon outing with friends and family or a romantic quiet time lingering by this restful spot with your favorite person these lovely falls make an ideal spot.

So grab a blanket…

Pack a well-filled basket…

Fill a thermos…

Come spend some quality (and mouth-watering!) time by the falls of the Carolinas.

Fresh Tomato Tart

Lemon pastry dough (see
accompanying recipe)
8 ounces mozzarella cheese, shredded
2 tablespoons chopped fresh basil
4-5 ripe tomatoes, cut into ½-inch slices

½ teaspoon salt
¼ teaspoon black pepper
¼ cup extra-virgin olive oil
Chopped fresh basil for garnish

- Preheat oven to 400°.
- Line a 10-inch loose-bottom tart pan with pastry dough. Spread bottom of pastry with cheese and sprinkle with basil. Cover with tomato slices, arranging to cover as evenly as possible. Sprinkle tomatoes with salt and pepper and drizzle with olive oil. Bake 30 to 40 minutes. Garnish with fresh chopped basil. Slice tart into wedges and serve warm or at room temperature.

Serves 4 to 6

Tomato Pie

1 (9-inch) pie shell
3-4 tomatoes, peeled and sliced
1 cup mayonnaise
1 cup grated sharp Cheddar cheese
1 cup grated mozzarella cheese

½ teaspoon black pepper
1 teaspoon garlic salt
1 teaspoon oregano
1 teaspoon basil
1 Vidalia onion, thinly sliced

- Preheat oven to 350°.
- Bake pie shell according to package directions.
- Slice tomatoes and drain on paper towels, turning once or twice to drain well. Combine mayonnaise, Cheddar and mozzarella cheese, pepper, garlic salt, oregano and basil.
- Layer tomatoes and onion in pie shell; spread mayonnaise mixture on top. Bake 30 minutes.
- Pie may be assembled in advance and stored in refrigerator until ready to bake.

Serves 6 to 8

Lemon Pastry Dough

1 cup all-purpose flour
½ cup unsalted butter, chilled
½ teaspoon salt
1 large egg yolk
2 teaspoons grated lemon zest

- In food processor, blend flour, butter, salt, egg yolk and lemon zest to a cornmeal-like consistency. Remove dough and knead lightly.
- Shape into ball, wrap and chill. Press into bottom of tart pan.

Makes 1 tart

Italian Tomato Casserole

2   (28-ounce) cans Italian-style diced tomatoes
2   tablespoons Italian seasoning
1   tablespoon oregano
1   tablespoon marjoram
1   tablespoon parsley
1   tablespoon allspice

1   tablespoon sage
1   medium onion, diced
1   teaspoon sugar
   Seasoned bread crumbs
1½ cups sharp Cheddar cheese
   Butter

- In a large saucepan, combine tomatoes, Italian seasoning, oregano, marjoram, parsley, allspice, sage, onion and sugar. Allow to stew on medium-low heat for about 1 hour.
- Preheat oven to 350°.
- Sprinkle enough bread crumbs into bottom of a 13 x 9 x 2-inch casserole dish to lightly cover bottom.
- Pour tomato mixture into casserole and cover with cheese. Add more bread crumbs to top and dot with butter.
- Bake 30 minutes.

Serves 8 to 10

Skillet Spinach

4   slices bacon
2½ tablespoons balsamic vinegar
1   (10-ounce) package fresh baby spinach, rinsed

2-3 tablespoons lightly toasted pecans, chopped
¼   teaspoon kosher salt
¼   teaspoon black pepper

- Cook bacon in a large skillet until crisp. Remove bacon and drain on paper towel, reserving 1 tablespoon drippings in skillet. Add vinegar to skillet. Bring to a boil over medium heat, stirring to loosen bacon particles.
- Add spinach and cook, stirring constantly, 1 to 2 minutes until wilted. Stir in bacon, pecans, salt and pepper.

Serves 4

Cabbage Casserole

6 tablespoons butter
2 cups cornflakes
4 cups shredded cabbage
1 small onion, minced
1 (8-ounce) can sliced water chestnuts

1 (10½-ounce) can cream of celery soup
1 cup milk
½ cup mayonnaise
Salt and pepper to taste
1 cup grated sharp Cheddar cheese

- Preheat oven to 350°.
- Melt butter and combine with cornflakes. Set aside.
- Grease a 9 x 13-inch casserole dish. Place cabbage in casserole dish. Top with onion and water chestnuts.
- Blend soup, milk, mayonnaise, salt and pepper and pour on top of casserole. Spread cheese over mixture.
- Top with buttered corn flakes. Bake 45 minutes.

Serves 6 to 8

Spinach and Artichoke Casserole

2 (10-ounce) packages frozen chopped spinach
2 (14-ounce) cans artichoke hearts
1 (8-ounce) package cream cheese, softened
1 stick margarine

1 tablespoon lemon juice
Dash hot sauce
Grated cheese (optional)
Bread crumbs (optional)

- Preheat oven to 350°.
- Cook spinach slightly and place in colander to drain. Slice artichoke hearts crosswise and place in bottom of lightly greased casserole dish.
- Combine cream cheese, margarine and drained spinach; add lemon juice and hot sauce. Pour spinach mixture over artichokes.
- Top with a little grated cheese and bread crumbs, if desired. Heat until bubbly.

Serves 6 to 8

Spinach Madeline

2   (10-ounce) packages frozen chopped spinach
4   tablespoons butter
2   tablespoons all-purpose flour
2   tablespoons finely chopped onion
½   cup evaporated milk
½   cup vegetable broth (reserved from cooked spinach)
½   teaspoon black pepper
¾   teaspoon celery salt

¾   teaspoon garlic salt (or ½ teaspoon minced garlic with ¼ teaspoon salt)
1   teaspoon Worcestershire sauce
    Crushed red pepper flakes to taste
8   ounces Monterey Jack cheese with peppers, cut into chunks for melting
¾   cup fresh bread crumbs
3   tablespoons butter, cut into small pieces

- Preheat oven to 300°.

- Cook spinach according to package directions, drain, reserving cooking liquid. Melt butter in saucepan over medium heat. Add flour and stir until smooth. Add onion and cook 2 minutes, stirring. Slowly add evaporated milk and spinach broth and whisk to remove any lumps. Cook 3 minutes or until smooth and thick. Add pepper, celery salt, garlic salt, Worcestershire, red pepper flakes and cheese, stirring until melted.

- Add spinach and combine well. Pour into 13 x 9 x 2-inch casserole dish and top with bread crumbs; dot with butter pieces. Bake 30 minutes.

Serves 6 to 8

Note: May prepare to baking point and refrigerate overnight to improve flavor and for convenience.

Spinach Squares

1	cup all-purpose flour
½	teaspoon salt
1	teaspoon baking soda
1	cup milk
2	eggs

½	cup chopped onion
¾-1	pound Cheddar cheese
1	(10-ounce) package frozen chopped spinach, thawed and drained well

- Preheat oven to 350°.
- Mix flour, salt, baking soda, milk and eggs with a fork. Fold in onion, cheese and spinach.
- Pour mixture into a 13 x 9 x 2-inch greased baking dish. Bake 30 to 35 minutes.
- Cool slightly before slicing into squares.

Makes 30 squares

Note: This makes 30 bite-size squares or you may slice larger and serve as a side dish for a meal.

Fresh Garden Delight

1	medium zucchini, sliced
1	medium yellow squash, sliced
1	medium onion, sliced
6-12	Chinese snow peas (if frozen, partially thawed)
1	cup fresh green beans, sliced

1	small bell pepper, chopped
4	tablespoons butter
¾	teaspoon seasoned salt
2	teaspoons ground pepper
½	teaspoon dried dill weed

- Sauté zucchini, squash, onion, pea pods, green beans and bell pepper in melted butter. Cover tightly for 10 to 12 minutes and stir occasionally. Sprinkle with seasoned salt, pepper and dill weed.

Serves 4

Collard Greens with Red Onions and Bacon

4   pounds collard greens
½   pound sliced bacon, cut crosswise into fourths
¼   cup cider vinegar
1¼ cups chicken broth

2   tablespoons firmly packed dark brown sugar
½   teaspoon dried hot pepper flakes
3   medium red onions, chopped coarsely

- Remove small leaves, coarse stems and ribs from collards and discard. Wash remaining leaves and stems well. Drain, chop coarsely and set aside.
- In a Dutch oven, cook bacon until crisp; drain on paper towel, reserving 3 tablespoons drippings in pot. Cook onions in drippings until soft.
- Add vinegar, broth, brown sugar, red pepper flakes and about half of bacon, stirring until sugar is dissolved.
- Add half the collards, tossing until slightly wilted. Add remaining collards, tossing until combined. Simmer greens 30 minutes.
- Stir in onions and simmer, covered, 30 minutes or until greens are tender. Top with bacon and serve.

Serves 8

Mushroom Bake

12 ounces fresh mushrooms
¼   cup chopped onion
½   stick butter
    Mixed herbs of choice

⅓   cup heavy cream
1   egg
2   egg yolks
1   cup grated Swiss cheese

- Preheat oven to 325°.
- In skillet, sauté mushrooms and onion in butter. Add herbs and cook about 4 minutes. In a bowl, combine cream, egg and egg yolks.
- Grease a 13 x 9 x 2-inch casserole dish and sprinkle bottom with Swiss cheese. Place mushroom mixture on top, then pour cream/egg mixture over all.
- Bake 30 minutes or until brown and bubbly.

Serves 4 to 6

Baked Yellow Squash with Spinach and Gruyère Cheese

2	medium yellow squash	¼	cup finely minced green onion
1	(10-ounce) package frozen chopped spinach	⅓	cup sour cream
	Salt and pepper to taste	¼	cup coarse bread crumbs
2	teaspoons butter	¼	shredded Gruyère or Swiss cheese

- Cut squash in half lengthwise, remove seeds and pulp, leaving a ¾-inch shell. Cook in microwave in a little water for 4 to 5 minutes. Drain upside down on paper towel.

- Cook spinach according to package directions and drain well, pressing out excess liquid with back of a spoon. Chop spinach coarsely and place in a bowl. Add salt, pepper, onion and sour cream.

- Preheat oven to 350°.

- Butter a casserole dish large enough to hold squash in one layer. Fill squash shells with spinach mixture; sprinkle with bread crumbs and cheese.

- Bake 15 to 20 minutes until bread crumbs are brown and squash is tender.

Serves 4

Squash Casserole

Casserole

2	cups cooked squash		½	teaspoon salt
1	cup milk		¼	teaspoon black pepper
1	small onion, chopped		1	cup bread crumbs
1	egg		¼	cup melted butter
½	cup grated sharp Cheddar Cheese			

- Preheat oven to 350°.

- Mix squash, milk, onion, eggs, cheese, salt, pepper and bread crumbs together in a mixing bowl.

- Pour into a greased 8 x 8 x 2-inch baking dish.

Topping

2	tablespoons butter, melted		½	cup grated sharp Cheddar cheese
½	cup bread crumbs			

- Melt butter and mix with bread crumbs; stir in cheese. Sprinkle on top of casserole.

- Bake 30 minutes.

Serves 4 to 6

Vidalia Onion Pie

6	tablespoons butter, divided	½	teaspoon salt
1	cup crushed buttery crackers	½	teaspoon black pepper
2	medium Vidalia onions, sliced and separated	½	cup shredded Cheddar or Swiss cheese
2	eggs, beaten		Paprika to taste
¾	cup milk		

- Preheat oven to 350°.
- Melt 4 tablespoons butter and combine with crackers. Press into 8-inch pie plate.
- Sauté onion in remaining butter until soft. In a bowl, combine eggs, milk, salt, pepper, cheese and paprika. Place onion in pie plate and top with egg and cheese mixture.
- Bake 30 minutes.

Serves 8

Savory Roasted New Potatoes

16	small red new potatoes, cut into large bite-size pieces	½	teaspoon salt
1	teaspoon minced fresh garlic	¼	teaspoon freshly ground black pepper
½	teaspoon paprika (hot variety, if available)	1	tablespoon Worcestershire sauce
2	tablespoons minced fresh rosemary	¼	cup olive oil

- Preheat oven to 375°.
- Place potatoes in large baking pan and sprinkle with garlic, paprika, rosemary, salt and pepper. Toss to combine.
- In a small bowl, combine Worcestershire and olive oil and drizzle over potatoes. Toss to coat.
- Bake in lower half of oven, stirring occasionally, 45 to 55 minutes or until browned and tender.

Serves 6 to 8

Goat Cheese and Thyme Potato Cake

1½ pounds small red potatoes
6 tablespoons unsalted butter, softened
½ cup sour cream

4 ounces goat cheese, preferably aged, grated
2 large eggs
1 teaspoon fresh thyme leaves

- Preheat oven to 375°.

- Generously oil or butter a 9 x 9 x 2-inch square baking pan and line with a 14 x 8-inch piece parchment paper, allowing ends of paper to overhang 2 opposite edges of pan. Press on paper to coat underside with oil or butter and turn over, keeping ends of paper overhanging.

- Cut potatoes into ¼-inch thick slices and in a pot of boiling salted water, cook until tender but not falling apart, about 8 minutes. Drain potatoes in a colander and cool 15 minutes.

- In a large bowl, whisk together butter and sour cream until smooth then whisk in goat cheese and eggs until well combined. Add potatoes, tossing gently, and transfer mixture to baking pan. Smooth top with a spatula, spreading potatoes evenly, and sprinkle with thyme. Bake potato cake in middle of oven 35 minutes, or until top is golden.

- Cool in pan on a rack. Potato cake may be made 2 days ahead and chilled, covered.

- Using parchment paper, lift potato cake from pan and transfer to a cutting board. Cut cake into squares, discarding parchment, and serve at room temperature.

Scalloped Potatoes

4 Idaho potatoes
1 clove garlic, cut in half
1 pint heavy cream
1 teaspoon salt

½ teaspoon black pepper
1 stick butter
½ cup shredded Swiss cheese
1 onion, thinly sliced

- Preheat oven to 325°.
- Peel potatoes and slice about ⅛-inch thick. Do not rinse.
- Rub garlic clove over surface of a casserole dish that is just big enough to hold potatoes (a 1-quart soufflé dish is best). Generously butter the dish.
- Heat heavy cream in a small saucepan to just below the simmer.
- Place ¼ of potatoes in an even layer, several slices thick, in the bottom of dish. Add enough cream to cover potatoes and season with salt and pepper. Dot with butter. Sprinkle with a small amount of cheese and onion. Repeat about 3 to 4 more times, ending with a layer of potatoes and cream (no cheese or onion on top) and dot with butter.
- Bake 60 to 90 minutes or until done (test with cake tester).

Serves 4 to 6

Garlic Green Beans

3 tablespoons olive oil
4 cloves garlic, minced
2 pounds fresh green beans, trimmed
½ cup chicken broth

1 teaspoon sugar
1¼ teaspoons salt
¼ teaspoon black pepper

- Heat oil in a large skillet until hot and sauté garlic over medium-high heat. Add beans, tossing to coat.
- Add broth, sugar, salt and pepper. Cover and reduce heat; simmer 10 minutes or until beans are crisp-tender.

Serves 4 to 6

Sweet Potato Soufflé

Soufflé

3	cups cooked, mashed sweet potatoes	2	eggs
1	cup sugar	½	cup milk
½	teaspoon salt	1	teaspoon vanilla extract
3	tablespoons margarine, melted		

• Preheat oven to 350°.

• Mix potatoes, sugar, salt, margarine, eggs, milk, and vanilla until well blended. Place into a buttered 1-quart soufflé dish.

Topping

1	cup light brown sugar	1	cup coconut
½	cup all-purpose flour	4	tablespoons margarine, melted
1	cup finely chopped pecans		

• In a deep bowl, combine sugar, flour, nuts, coconut and margarine and mix well. Sprinkle over soufflé.

• Bake 25 minutes.

Serves 4 to 6

Swiss Green Bean Bake

2   (10-ounce) packages frozen French-style green beans,
      or 3 (14½-ounce) cans

3   tablespoons butter

3   tablespoons all-purpose flour

1   teaspoon salt

2   teaspoons sugar

4   teaspoons finely chopped onion

1   cup sour cream

8   ounces grated Swiss cheese

     Fresh bread crumbs or cracker crumbs

     Butter

- Preheat oven to 350°.
- Cook green beans according to package directions; drain and place in a medium casserole dish.
- Melt butter in saucepan over medium heat and whisk in flour. Stir and cook for 3 minutes, making a light brown roux. Add salt and sugar.
- Remove from heat and add onion, sour cream and cheese. Pour mixture over beans. Top with bread or cracker crumbs and dot with small pieces of butter.
- Bake 20 to 30 minutes or until top is lightly browned.

Serves 6

Sesame Noodles

½   pound dry Asian egg noodles

2   tablespoons soy sauce

2   cloves garlic, chopped

1   teaspoon hot pepper flakes

1   teaspoon sesame oil

¼   cup vegetable oil

- In a large stockpot over high heat, bring 2 quarts water to a boil. Add noodles and cook 4 to 5 minutes, or until al dente. Put drained noodles into a serving bowl and set aside.
- In a small bowl, whisk together soy sauce, garlic, pepper flakes, sesame oil and vegetable oil until well blended and pour over noodles.
- May be served warm or at room temperature.

Serves 6

Green Bean and Tomato Salad with Bacon and Pine Nut Dressing

¼ cup pine nuts

6 ounces smoked bacon

1¼ pounds fresh green beans, trimmed

2 medium tomatoes, cut into wedges

3 tablespoons extra-virgin olive oil

3 tablespoons red wine vinegar

½ teaspoon sugar

½ teaspoon salt

¼ teaspoon freshly ground black pepper

- Preheat oven to 375°.

- Spread pine nuts on a baking sheet, toast in oven until golden brown, about 10 minutes. Set aside.

- Cook bacon until crisp and crumble; reserving 2 tablespoons drippings.

- In a large saucepan of boiling water, cook beans, stirring once, about 5 minutes. Drain immediately and rinse beans under cold water. Drain again thoroughly and arrange on platter.

- Place tomato wedges around beans.

- In a small skillet, heat bacon drippings and olive oil. Stir in vinegar, sugar, salt and pepper. Bring to a boil and simmer 1 minute, stirring until sugar dissolves. Add pine nuts. Pour over beans.

Serves 4

Cauliflower Home Style

1	head cauliflower, cut into 1-inch florets	2	large eggs
2	tablespoons fresh bread crumbs	2	tablespoons sour cream
1	tablespoon unsalted butter	1	cup shredded mozzarella cheese

- Preheat oven to 375° and lightly butter 2-quart baking dish.

- In a kettle of boiling salted water, cook cauliflower 3 minutes and drain well.

- In a large nonstick skillet, sauté bread crumbs in butter over moderate-high heat, stirring until golden. Stir in cauliflower and remove from heat.

- In a large bowl, whisk together eggs, sour cream, and cheese. Add cauliflower mixture, stirring to combine well. Transfer mixture to a baking dish and bake 25 minutes or until pale golden.

Serves 4 to 6

Mustard-Topped Cauliflower

1	head cauliflower, rinsed	¼	teaspoon salt
½	cup water	⅔	cup shredded Swiss or Cheddar cheese
½	cup mayonnaise		Paprika for garnish
1	tablespoon finely chopped onion		
2	teaspoons prepared mustard		

- In a deep microwave-safe casserole dish, place whole cauliflower head with water. Cover with plastic wrap and cut a slit in center to vent. Microwave on HIGH 10 to 15 minutes. Drain.

- Meanwhile, combine mayonnaise, onion, mustard and salt. Pour over hot cauliflower. Sprinkle cheese over sauce and top with a sprinkle of paprika. Cook in microwave on HIGH, uncovered, 2 minutes.

Serves 4 to 6

Philly Sauce Supreme

½ cup milk

1 (8-ounce) package cream cheese, cubed

¼ cup Parmesan cheese

½ teaspoon onion salt

- Heat milk and cream cheese over low heat, stirring until smooth. Blend in Parmesan cheese and onion salt.

- Serve over hot cooked vegetables.

Broccoli Puffs

2	(10-ounce) packages chopped broccoli	1	tablespoon butter, softened
3	eggs, separated	¼	teaspoon salt
1	tablespoon all-purpose flour	¼	teaspoon black pepper
	Pinch nutmeg	¼	cup plus 1 tablespoon grated Parmesan cheese
1	cup mayonnaise		

- Preheat oven to 350°.

- Cook broccoli, drain well.

- Beat egg yolks; add flour, mixing well. Stir in nutmeg, mayonnaise, butter, salt, pepper and cheese. Add broccoli, mixing lightly.

- Beat egg whites until stiff peaks form; gently fold into broccoli mixture. Pour into a lightly buttered 9 x 9 x 2-inch square baking dish.

- Bake 30 minutes. Cut into squares.

Makes 16 squares

Carrot Souffle

2	pounds carrots, boiled and mashed	1	teaspoon baking powder
½	cup butter	¾	cup sugar
2	eggs, beaten		Pinch ground cinnamon
3	tablespoons all-purpose flour		

- Preheat oven to 400°.

- Combine carrots, butter, eggs, flour, baking powder, sugar and cinnamon and pour into a buttered 1-quart souffle dish.

- Bake 15 minutes. Reduce oven to 350° and bake an additional 45 minutes.

Serves 12

Broccoli with Orange Sauce

1	bunch fresh broccoli	½	teaspoon grated orange zest
2	tablespoons butter	¼	teaspoon dried tarragon
2	tablespoons all-purpose flour	¼	teaspoon salt
½	cup orange juice	½	plain yogurt
½	cup orange sections		

- Separate broccoli into spears, removing any tough stems. Cook broccoli, covered, in a small amount of boiling water 10 minutes or until crisp-tender.
- Melt butter in a heavy saucepan over low heat; add flour and cook 1 minute, stirring constantly. Gradually stir in juice. Stir in orange sections and zest, tarragon and salt; cook over medium heat, stirring constantly, until thickened and bubbly. Stir in yogurt.
- Drain broccoli and arrange on a serving platter. Spoon sauce over top.

Serves 4

Zesty Baked Carrots

6-8	carrots, cut lengthwise and in 2- or 3-inch pieces	½	teaspoon salt
¼	cup water	¼	teaspoon black pepper
2	tablespoons grated onion	¼	cup cracker crumbs
2	tablespoons horseradish	1	tablespoon butter
½	cup mayonnaise		Dash paprika

- Preheat oven to 375°.
- Slice carrots and cook until tender. Place in a shallow casserole dish. Mix water, onion, horseradish, mayonnaise, salt and pepper. Pour over carrots.
- Mix cracker crumbs with butter and sprinkle over carrots. Sprinkle with paprika.
- Bake 15 to 20 minutes.

Serves 6

Mimosa Sauce for Steamed Broccoli

3 tablespoons mayonnaise

1 teaspoon orange juice

- Whisk together mayonnaise and juice. Serve over broccoli or asparagus.

Perfect Glazed Carrots

1   pound carrots (about 6 medium)
½   teaspoon salt
3   tablespoons sugar, divided
½   cup chicken broth

1   tablespoon butter, cut into 4 pieces
2   tablespoons lemon juice
    Freshly ground black pepper

- Peel carrots and slice ¼-inch thick on the bias.
- In a 12-inch, nonstick skillet, bring carrots, salt, 1 tablespoon sugar and broth to boil over medium-high heat. Reduce heat to medium and simmer, stirring occasionally, until carrots are almost tender when tested with tip of paring knife, about 5 minutes.
- Uncover, increase heat to high, and simmer rapidly 1 to 2 minutes, stirring occasionally, until liquid is reduced to about 2 tablespoons. Add butter and remaining sugar to skillet; toss carrots to coat and cook, stirring frequently, until carrots are completely tender and glaze is lightly golden, about 3 minutes.
- Remove from heat, add lemon juice and toss to coat. Transfer carrots to serving dish, scraping glaze from pan. Season to taste with pepper and serve immediately.

Glazed Carrots with Ginger and Rosemary

1   teaspoon minced fresh rosemary

1   (1-inch) piece fresh ginger

- Cut ginger crosswise into ¼-inch coins. Follow recipe above, adding ginger to skillet along with carrots and adding rosemary along with butter. Discard ginger pieces before serving.

Honey-Glazed Carrots with Lemon and Thyme

3   tablespoons honey
½   teaspoon minced fresh thyme

½   teaspoon grated lemon zest

- Follow recipe for Perfect Glazed Carrots, substitute honey for sugar and adding thyme and lemon zest along with butter.

Glazed Curried Carrots with Currants and Almonds

¼   cup sliced almonds
1½ teaspoons curry powder

¼   cup currants

Perfect Glazed Carrots continued

- Toast almonds in 12-inch nonstick skillet over medium heat until fragrant and lightly browned, about 5 minutes; transfer to small bowl and set aside.
- Remove skillet from heat and sprinkle curry powder in skillet; stir until fragrant, about 2 seconds, to bring forth curry's full flavor.
- Follow recipe for Perfect Glazed Carrots, adding carrots, salt, sugar and broth to skillet with curry powder.
- Add currants along with butter; add toasted almonds along with lemon juice.

Serves 6

Chili Cheese Rice

1	cup chopped onion	1	teaspoon salt
¼	cup butter, melted	¼	teaspoon black pepper
4	cups cooked long-grain rice	2	(4½-ounce) cans chopped green chiles
1	(16-ounce) carton sour cream	2	cups shredded Cheddar or Monterey Jack cheese
1	cup ricotta cheese		

- Preheat oven to 325°. Lightly grease a 2-quart casserole dish.
- In a large saucepan, saute onion in butter. Remove from heat; stir in rice, sour cream, ricotta cheese, salt, pepper and chiles.
- Spoon half of rice mixture into casserole. Top with half of cheese. Top with remaining rice mixture. Bake, uncovered, 20 minutes; sprinkle with remaining cheese and bake 5 minutes or until cheese is melted.

Serves 6

Spicy Baked Rice

1	cup long-grain rice, uncooked	⅔	cup pimiento-stuffed olives, sliced
2	(10-ounce) cans diced tomatoes and green chiles, undrained	¼	cup olive oil
		½	cup chopped onion
1	cup water	1	cup shredded Monterey Jack cheese

- Preheat oven to 350°.

- In a shallow 2-quart baking dish, combine rice, tomatoes and chiles, water, olives, oil, onion and cheese.

- Bake, covered, 45 minutes. Stir well and bake, uncovered, 15 additional minutes or until liquid is absorbed and rice is tender.

Serves 4

Saffron Rice with Black Beans

1	large onion, diced	1	tablespoon red wine vinegar
2	cloves garlic, minced	1	teaspoon sugar
2	tablespoons olive oil	½	teaspoon salt
3	(15-ounce) cans black beans, rinsed and drained	1	(8-ounce) can tomato sauce
1	(14½-ounce) can Cajun-style stewed tomatoes, chopped, reserving liquid		Cooked saffron rice
			Chopped green onions for garnish
1½	cups water		Sour cream for garnish

- Saute onion and garlic in olive oil in a Dutch oven over medium heat, stirring constantly, until tender. Add beans, tomatoes, water, vinegar, sugar, salt and tomato sauce; bring mixture to a boil. Cover, reduce heat, and simmer 1 hour.

- Uncover and simmer 20 to 30 minutes, stirring occasionally.

- Serve black bean mixture over hot cooked rice. Top each serving with green onions and a dollop of sour cream.

Serves 8

Apricot Rice

3	tablespoons butter		2	(14½-ounce) cans chicken broth
¼	cup pine nuts or almonds		½	cup sliced green onions
1¼	cups raw rice		½	cup dried, diced apricots

- Melt butter in skillet. Saute nuts for 2 minutes, remove nuts with slotted spoon. Add rice to butter; stir for 3 to 5 minutes. Stir in 1 can broth, then the remaining broth.
- Simmer 30 minutes. Add nuts, onions and apricots. Cover and cook 5 minutes.

Serves 4

Orzo Pilaf

3	cups chicken broth		1	clove garlic, minced
1	cup orzo		½	cup grated carrots
4	slices bacon		2	tablespoons finely diced red bell pepper
½	cup chopped onion		2	tablespoons finely diced green bell pepper

- Bring broth to a boil; stir in pasta. Boil about 10 minutes or until tender; drain. Meanwhile, cook bacon in a large skillet until crisp. Remove from skillet, crumble, and set aside. Drain pan, reserving 3 tablespoons of drippings in skillet.
- Cook and stir onion and garlic in reserved drippings until tender but not browned. Add pasta, carrots and bell peppers. Heat thoroughly, tossing constantly to coat. Sprinkle with bacon.

Serves 8

Rice Pilaf with Pepper, Peas and Asparagus

Rice

1	tablespoon butter		¼	teaspoon fresh or dried thyme
1	cup chopped onions		1	bay leaf
1½	cups long-grain white rice			Salt and freshly ground pepper to taste
3	cups chicken stock			

- Melt butter in a saucepan over medium heat. Stir in onion and cook a few minutes to soften. Add rice and stir well to coat rice with butter.

- Pour in chicken stock; add thyme, bay leaf, salt and pepper. Bring to a boil. Cover with tight-fitting lid, reduce heat to very low, and cook 15 to 20 minutes, until rice is tender and all liquid has been absorbed. You may serve the pilaf plain at this point.

- While rice is cooking, prepare vegetable garnish.

Vegetable Garnish

1	tablespoon olive oil		½	cup fresh or frozen green peas
½	cup red bell pepper, diced			Salt and pepper to taste
½	cup fresh asparagus, cut into 1-inch pieces			

- In a saute pan over medium heat, add oil, bell pepper, asparagus and green peas; toss together. Add about 4 tablespoons of water, sprinkle with salt and pepper.

- Bring water to a boil, cover pan, and cook for about 5 minutes or until done. Check water level once or twice, adding a little if necessary.

- Spoon vegetables over rice and toss together. Serve immediately.

Serves 6 to 8

Orzo with Leeks

¾	cup orzo		⅛	teaspoon salt
1	tablespoon butter		1	clove garlic
4	ounces mushrooms (or zucchini)		¼	cup water
1	leek, sliced		¼	teaspoon marjoram
¼	teaspoon black pepper		½	teaspoon chicken bouillon granules

- Cook orzo according to package directions. Cook leek and mushroom and garlic in butter until tender. Add salt and pepper. Add water, bouillon and marjoram. Toss with orzo.
- Serve with grated or sliced Parmesan cheese.

Serves 4

Tortellini with Tomatoes and Corn

1	(9-ounce) package cheese tortellini		¼	cup fresh basil
1	(10-ounce) package frozen corn		2	tablespoons Parmesan cheese
1	clove garlic, halved		1	teaspoon olive oil
2	cups cherry tomatoes		⅛	teaspoon black pepper
¼	cup sliced green onions			

- Cook tortellini in boiling water according to package directions. Do not add salt or oil. Add corn and cook for additional 3 minutes. Drain well. Rub bowl with garlic clove. Add tomatoes, onion, basil, cheese, oil and pepper; toss well.

Serves 6

Risotto with Parmigiano and Asparagus Tips

6   cups chicken broth, preferably homemade
5   tablespoons unsalted butter, divided
1   small onion, finely minced
2   cups imported Arborio rice
1   cup dry white wine

1½ pounds fresh, thin asparagus, cleaned, tips cut off,
       saving stalks for another purpose
    Salt to taste
½   cup freshly grated Parmigiano-Reggiano cheese

- Heat broth in a medium saucepan and keep warm over low heat.

- In a separate large saucepan, melt 4 tablespoons butter over medium heat. When butter foams, add onion and cook, stirring, for 3 to 4 minutes, until onion is soft. Add rice and cook until it is well coated with butter and onion. Add wine and cook, stirring constantly, until wine is almost all reduced. Add just enough hot broth to barely cover rice.

- Cook, still over medium heat, stirring constantly, until broth has been absorbed almost completely. Add more broth as the liquid is absorbed, continually stirring. After 6 to 7 minutes of cooking, add asparagus tips. Continue cooking and stirring rice, adding broth a bit at a time, until rice is tender, but still firm to the bite, another 7 to 8 minutes.

- Season with salt. Stir in remaining butter and cheese.

- Mix well and quickly to blend. At this point, rice should have a moist, creamy, and somewhat loose consistency. Serve at once with a sprinkling of additional Parmigiano cheese.

Serves 6 to 8

Sweets

Sunset at the Upper Falls
South Mountain

Hundreds of years ago two great Native American tribes, the Cherokees and the Catawbas, dwelled in the valleys and mountain ranges of the Blue Ridge where the great Catawba River flowed. A rugged expanse of peaks called the South Mountains served as boundary lines between these two groups. As years passed, European settlers wandered into this fertile area to establish prosperous farms. Before long, gold was discovered in these North Carolina Mountains; causing a gold rush some twenty years before the great California Gold Rush. Now the years of gold and pioneers have passed, but many still come to revel in the exquisite landscape of the South Mountains. Travel to the Upper Falls and watch as the day fades into a glowing sunset. Gold and pink hues bathe the surrounding terrain. It is truly a feast for the eyes. And after a day of treating your other senses, reward your palate with an equally awe-inspiring selection from the following pages.

Warm Chocolate Cakes

4   ounces semi-sweet chocolate, chopped
1½ ounces unsweetened chocolate, chopped
1¼ sticks unsalted butter, softened
½   cup plus 2 tablespoons sugar

3   eggs, lightly beaten
½   cup plus 2 teaspoons all-purpose flour
1½ tablespoons cocoa powder
¾   teaspoon baking powder

- Coat six ¾- to 1-cup ramekins lightly with butter. Combine semi-sweet chocolate and unsweetened chocolate in the top of a double boiler. Heat over barely simmering water until smooth, stirring constantly. Add unsalted butter and sugar. Heat until butter melts and sugar dissolves, stirring frequently. Pour chocolate mixture into a large mixing bowl.

- Add eggs, flour, cocoa and baking powder to chocolate mixture and mix well. Beat for 8 minutes or until thickened to a mousse consistency. Spoon chocolate mixture evenly into prepared ramekins. Freeze, covered with plastic wrap, for 3 hours or longer. You may prepare up to this point 3 days in advance; remove plastic wrap.

- Arrange ramekins on a baking sheet. Place baking sheet on center oven rack. Bake at 375° for 14 minutes or until the edges are set and tops are moist and shiny. Do not overbake. Let stand for 10 minutes. Invert onto individual dessert plates. Serve warm with ice cream or whipped cream.

Serves 6

Basic White Cake

½ cup butter
½ cup shortening
2 cups sugar
3 cups cake flour
4 teaspoons baking powder

½ teaspoon salt
⅔ cup milk
⅔ cup water
2 teaspoons vanilla extract
¾ teaspoon almond extract
6 egg whites

- Preheat oven to 325°.

- Beat butter and shortening until creamy. Add sugar; beat well.

- Combine flour, baking powder and salt then add alternately with milk and water. Beat at low speed until blended. Stir in extracts.

- Beat egg whites at high speed with electric mixer until stiff peaks form; fold ⅓ of whites into batter. Gradually fold in remaining egg whites.

- Pour into three greased 10-inch round cake pans. Bake 18 to 22 minutes.

Serves 24

Orange Cream Cake

1   recipe Basic White Cake Batter (see page 204)
    Orange Cream Filling (recipe follows)

1   recipe Orange Buttercream Frosting (recipe follows)

- Bake three 9-inch white cakes.
- Spread Orange Cream filling between cake layers (not on top). Cover and chill at least 4 hours.
- Spread Orange Buttercream Frosting on top and sides of cake. Store in refrigerator. Cake may be frozen up to one month.

Orange Cream Filling

½   cup sugar
6   tablespoons cornstarch
6   egg yolks
2   cups half & half

3   tablespoons butter, cut up
3   tablespoons orange liqueur or orange juice concentrate
2   tablespoons grated orange zest
1   teaspoon vanilla extract

- Combine first four ingredients in a 3-quart saucepan. Bring to a boil over medium heat, whisking constantly. Boil for one minute or until thickened, continuing to whisk. Remove from heat, whisk in butter, 3 tablespoons orange liqueur, orange zest and vanilla. Cover and chill at least four hours.

Orange Buttercream Frosting

½   cup butter, softened
1   (16-ounce) package confectioners' sugar
3   tablespoons orange liqueur
3   tablespoons milk

2   tablespoons orange rind
1   drop red food coloring
1   drop yellow food coloring
1   teaspoon vanilla extract

- Beat butter at medium speed with an electric mixer until creamy; gradually add 1 cup confectioners' sugar, beating at low speed until blended.
- Add remaining ingredients, beating until blended. Gradually add remaining confectioners' sugar.

Lemon Meringue Cake

---

1 recipe Basic White Cake Batter (see page 204)	Lemon Filling (recipe follows)

- Bake three 9-inch white cakes

- Spread Lemon Filling between layers. Cover and chill at least 4 hours.

- Spread with Meringue frosting on top and sides.

Lemon Filling

1½	cups sugar	2½	cups half & half
½	cup cornstarch	¼	cup butter, cut up
¼	teaspoon salt	1	tablespoon grated lemon zest
6	egg yolks	¾	cup fresh lemon juice

- In a 3-quart saucepan, combine sugar, cornstarch, salt, egg yolks and half & half over medium heat, whisking constantly. Bring to a boil and whisk 1 minute until thickened. Remove from heat, whisk in lemon juice until smooth; pour into a bowl.

- Cover and chill at least 4 hours.

Meringue Frosting

3	tablespoons meringue powder (found at cake supply stores)	¼	teaspoon cream of tartar
½	cup water	½	cup sugar

- Beat meringue powder and water with electric mixer on high until foamy. Add cream of tartar, beating until soft peaks form. Gradually add sugar, 1 tablespoon at a time, beating until stiff peaks form.

- Before frosting cake with Meringue Frosting, you need to heat oven to 425°. Frost top and sides of cake with Meringue Frosting.

- Place in oven for 10 minutes or until golden. (Top will brown more than sides.)

Serves 16

Autumn Cake

3   eggs
2⅔ cups sugar
1½ cups oil
3   cups all-purpose flour
2   teaspoons ground cinnamon
1   teaspoon soda

1   teaspoon salt
1   teaspoon vanilla extract
1   cup shredded carrots
1   cup shredded coconut
1   cup chopped pecans
1   (18-ounce) can crushed pineapple

- Preheat oven to 325°.

- Drain pineapple and set aside.

- Combine eggs, sugar and oil in large mixing bowl. Sift flour, cinnamon, soda and salt together. Slowly add to egg mixture. Stir in vanilla. Add carrots, coconut, pecans and pineapple; mix well.

- Pour batter into greased and floured tube or Bundt pan. Bake 1½ hours. Cool cake before removing from pan.

Serves 16

Upside-Down Pear Gingerbread Cake

Topping

2½ firm pears, preferably Bosc

¼ cup unsalted butter

¾ cup packed light brown sugar

- Peel and core pears and cut each into 8 wedges.

- Melt butter in skillet over moderate heat. Reduce heat to low and sprinkle brown sugar over bottom of skillet; cook undisturbed for 3 minutes. Not all sugar will be melted.

- Arrange pears decoratively over sugar and cook, undisturbed, for 2 minutes. Remove from heat and set aside.

Cake

2½ cups all-purpose flour

1½ teaspoons baking soda

1 teaspoon ground cinnamon

1 teaspoon ground ginger

¼ teaspoon salt

Vanilla ice cream for serving

1 cup light molasses

1 cup boiling water

½ cup unsalted butter, softened

½ cup packed light brown sugar

1 large egg, lightly beaten

- Preheat oven to 350°. In large bowl, whisk together flour, baking soda, cinnamon, ginger and salt in a bowl.

- In a separate small bowl, mix together molasses and water.

- In another large bowl, beat together butter, brown sugar, and egg with an electric mixer at medium speed until creamy, about 2 minutes.

- Alternately mix in flour mixture and molasses into butter mixture in 3 batches, with electric mixer on low speed, until smooth.

- Pour batter over topping in skillet, spreading evenly and being careful not to disturb pears.

- Bake in middle of oven 40 to 50 minutes, or until a knife inserted in the center comes out clean.

- Cool cake in skillet on a rack 5 minutes. Run a thin knife around edge of skillet, then invert on a large plate. Replace any pears that stick to skillet.

- Serve warm or at room temperature, with a scoop of ice cream.

Serves 6

Special Equipment: a well-seasoned 10-inch cast iron skillet or a 12-inch deep nonstick skillet (handle wrapped with a double layer of foil if not ovenproof).

One Pan Fudge Cake

2	cups sugar	½	cup oil
2	cups all-purpose flour	3-4	tablespoons cocoa
1	teaspoon baking soda	½	cup buttermilk
1	teaspoon ground cinnamon	1	teaspoon vanilla extract
1	cup water	2	eggs, slightly beaten
1	stick butter		

- Preheat oven to 350°.
- In a mixing bowl, combine sugar, flour, baking soda and cinnamon and set aside.
- In a saucepan, mix water, butter, oil and cocoa then bring to a boil. Add flour mixture.
- Add buttermilk, vanilla and eggs to cocoa mixture.
- Pour into greased and floured 13 x 9 x 2-inch baking dish. Bake 30 minutes (or 400° for 20 minutes).

Frosting

1	stick butter	1	box confectioners' sugar
6	tablespoons evaporated milk	1	cup chopped nuts
4	tablespoons cocoa	1	teaspoon vanilla extract

- In a saucepan, bring butter, milk and cocoa to a boil; remove from heat.
- Add sugar, nuts and vanilla to boiled cocoa mixture and pour over warm cake.

Symphony Bar Brownies

1 deluxe brownie mix

3 large Symphony candy bars

3 eggs

Confectioners' sugar

- Make sure brownie mix is for 13 x 9 x 2-inch pan.
- Preheat oven to temperature as directed on brownie mix package.
- Cook as directed on package, using the extra egg recipe. Pour half the batter into a greased 13 x 9 x 2-inch pan; then place candy on top. Pour remaining half of batter over candy. Bake according to package directions.
- Cut with plastic knife. Sprinkle with confectioners' sugar.

Note: You may use your favorite brownie recipe, but they are simply delicious as above.

Serves 12 to 16

Jewish Apple Cake

6	medium apples, Granny Smith or Golden Delicious, thinly sliced	1	cup oil
5	tablespoons sugar plus 2 cups, divided	4	eggs
2	teaspoons ground cinnamon	⅓	cup orange juice
3	cups all-purpose flour	1	tablespoon baking powder
		1	teaspoon salt

- Preheat oven to 350°.

- Peel and core apples and slice thinly.

- Mix 5 tablespoons sugar and cinnamon in a plastic bag. Add apples and toss to coat with mixture.

- In a bowl, combine flour, oil, eggs, orange juice, baking powder and salt then mix until smooth.

- Pour half of batter into a greased and floured (or sugared) tube pan, and distribute half the apples over top. Pour other half of batter on top, and distribute remaining apples over top.

- Bake 90 minutes, until cake pulls away from sides of pan.

- Cool 10 minutes, then invert. Invert again onto a serving plate, with the apple layer on top.

Serves 16

Lemon Whipping Cream Pound Cake

2	sticks butter	½	teaspoon baking powder
3	cups sugar	¼	teaspoon salt
5	eggs	1	teaspoon lemon extract
3	cups all-purpose flour	1	(8-ounce) carton whipping cream

- Preheat oven to 325°.

- Mix butter and sugar together and beat well. Add eggs, one at a time.

- Add half the flour, baking powder, salt, extract. Mix and add whipping cream and remaining flour, mix thoroughly. Pour into prepared tube pan.

- Bake 1 hour and 15 minutes.

- Cool and serve.

Serves 16

Frozen Mocha Cheesecake

1¼	cups chocolate wafer cookie crumbs (approximately 24 cookies)	1	(14-ounce) can sweetened condensed milk
¼	cup sugar	⅔	cup chocolate syrup
¼	cup margarine, melted	2	tablespoons instant coffee
1	(8-ounce) package cream cheese	1	teaspoon hot water
		1	cup whipping cream, whipped

- Combine cookie crumbs, sugar and margarine. In buttered springform pan, pat crumbs firmly on bottom and up the sides. Chill.

- In a large mixing bowl, beat cream cheese until fluffy. Add condensed milk.

- Dissolve coffee in water. Mix well. Fold in whipped cream.

- Pour into prepared pan. Cover and freeze 6 hours or until firm. Garnish with additional crumbs.

Serves 18

Note: Must keep leftovers in freezer.

Chocolate Glazed Bailey's Irish Cream Cheesecake

6   whole graham crackers, finely crushed
½   stick butter, melted
3   (8-ounce) packages cream cheese, softened
7   tablespoons sugar
1   tablespoon all-purpose flour
2   large eggs

¼   cup plus 2 tablespoons sour cream
¼   cup plus 2 tablespoons Bailey's Irish Cream
1   teaspoon vanilla extract
½   cup whipping cream
9   ounces semi-sweet chocolate, chopped

- Preheat oven to 350°.

- Combine graham cracker crumbs and melted butter. Press onto bottom (not sides) of 9-inch springform pan. Bake about 8 minutes, until golden brown.

- Using electric mixer, beat cream cheese and sugar until smooth. Beat in flour. Add eggs, one at a time, beating until just combined. Mix in sour cream, Bailey's Irish Cream and vanilla extract. Pour filling into crust.

- Bake 10 minutes. Reduce oven temperature to 250° and bake 40 minutes longer until cake is set. Cool on rack 10 minutes.

- Run knife around pan sides to loosen cake. Chill overnight.

- Bring whipping cream to simmer. Reduce heat to low. Add chocolate and stir until melted and smooth. Cool glaze to lukewarm.

- Release pan sides from cake and place cake on a rack. Pour glaze over cake, spreading to cover top and sides and allowing excess to drip under rack. Refrigerate until set, at least 30 minutes.

Serves 18

Chocolate Amaretto Cheesecake

6   chocolate wafers, crushed
1½ cups light cream cheese
1   cup sugar
1   cup 1% low-fat cottage cheese
¼   cup plus 2 tablespoons unsweetened cocoa
¼   cup all-purpose flour

¼   cup amaretto
1   teaspoon vanilla extract
¼   teaspoon salt
1   egg
2   tablespoons semi-sweet mini chocolate morsels
    Chocolate curls

- Preheat oven to 300°.
- Sprinkle crumbs in 7-inch springform pan.
- Position knife in food processor. Add cream cheese, sugar, cottage cheese, cocoa, flour, amaretto, vanilla and salt. Combine until smooth. Add egg and process just until blended.
- Fold in chocolate morsels.
- Slowly pour mixture over crumbs in pan.
- Bake 65 to 70 minutes or until set.
- Cover and chill at least 8 hours. Remove pan.
- Garnish with chocolate curls (3 squares semi-sweet chocolate).

Serves 18

Chocolate Charm Almond Pie

5	chocolate with almond candy bars	1	cup whipping cream, whipped
18	marshmallows	1	(9-inch) pie shell, baked
½	cup milk		

- Combine candy bars, marshmallows and milk in a heavy saucepan. Cook over low heat, stirring occasionally, until melted. Remove from heat; cool.
- Fold in whipped cream. Pour into pastry shell. Chill at least 8 hours.

Makes 1 pie

Sweet Potato Pie

2	(14-ounce) cans sweet potatoes, drained and mashed	1	teaspoon vanilla extract
2	cups sugar	¼	teaspoon nutmeg
1	stick butter or margarine, melted	1	teaspoon ground cinnamon (optional)
4	eggs	2	(9-inch) pie shells, unbaked
½	cup evaporated milk		

- Preheat oven to 350°.
- In a large mixing bowl, blend sweet potatoes, sugar and margarine. Add eggs and milk, mixing with electric mixer until large pieces of potato are gone. Add nutmeg, vanilla and cinnamon (if using) and mix well.
- Pour into 2 unbaked 9-inch pie shells. Bake 55 to 60 minutes, until center is done.

Makes 2 pies

Upside-Down Apple Pecan Pie

1 cup chopped pecans
½ cup firmly packed brown sugar
⅓ cup margarine or butter, melted
2 (9-inch) pie crusts
6 medium apples, sliced and peeled

¼ cup sugar
2 tablespoons all-purpose flour
½ teaspoon ground cinnamon
⅛ teaspoon nutmeg

- Preheat oven to 375°.

- In 9-inch pie pan, combine pecans, brown sugar and margarine; spread evenly over bottom of pan. Prepare pie crusts for two-crust pie, placing bottom crust over pecan mixture in pan.

- In large bowl, combine apples, sugar, flour, cinnamon and nutmeg; mix lightly. Spoon into pie crust-lined pan. Top with second crust and flute; cut slits in several places.

- Bake 40 to 50 minutes or until crust is golden brown and apples are tender. (Place pan on foil or cookie sheet during baking to guard against spillage.)

- Cool pie upright in pan for 5 minutes. Place serving plate over pie; invert. Carefully remove pan. Some nuts may remain in pan; replace on pie with knife.

- Cool at least 1 hour before serving. Garnish as desired.

Serves 8

Tiramisu Toffee Trifle Pie

1	(10¾-ounce) frozen loaf pound cake, thawed	¾	cup warm water
1	(12-ounce) carton frozen whipped topping, thawed	½	cup confectioners' sugar
1	(8-ounce) package cream cheese, softened	½	cup chocolate syrup
1½	tablespoons instant coffee	2	(1.4-ounce) Heath Bars, coarsely chopped

- Allow pound cake and frozen whipped topping to thaw at room temperature. Allow cream cheese to soften.

- Mix instant coffee with water and allow to cool.

- Cut cake into 14 slices, then cut these slices in half diagonally. Line a 9-inch deep-dish pie pan with cake, making sure cake covers the entire bottom and sides of pan. Drizzle coffee over cake, being sure to cover all the cake with coffee.

- Beat cream cheese, sugar and syrup until smooth. Add 2½ cups whipped topping and fold gently until combined. Spread over cake. Sprinkle candy pieces over top. Chill for 8 hours.

- To serve, put chocolate syrup in a squeeze bottle and make a swirly design with syrup on each serving plate. Top with a pie slice.

Serves 8 to 10

Tar Heel Pie

1	cup chocolate chips	½	cup sugar
½	cup margarine, melted	½	cup brown sugar
1	cup chopped pecans	2	eggs, beaten
1	teaspoon vanilla extract	1	(9-inch) pie shell, unbaked
½	cup all-purpose flour		

- Preheat oven to 350°.

- Pour warm margarine over chocolate chips and stir.

- In a separate bowl, mix pecans, vanilla, flour, sugars and eggs until well blended. Stir pecan mixture into chocolate mixture. Pour into pie shell.

- Bake 30 to 40 minutes.

Makes 1 pie

Chocolate-Pecan Whiskey Pie

6 ounces semi-sweet chocolate
3 tablespoons butter
1 (9-inch) pie shell
2 eggs
¾ cup sugar
¼ cup light corn syrup

¼ cup whiskey
1 cup chopped pecans
Whipped cream for garnish (optional)
Shaved chocolate for garnish (optional)
Chocolate-dipped pecan halves for garnish (optional)

- Preheat oven to 350°.
- In a medium, heavy saucepan, melt chocolate and butter over low heat, stirring frequently. Remove from heat and cool.
- In a mixing bowl, beat eggs, sugar, syrup and whiskey until smooth. Slowly stir egg mixture into chocolate. Stir in pecans.
- Pour chocolate-pecan mixture into pastry shell. To prevent over-browning, cover edge of pie with foil. Bake 25 minutes. Remove foil and continue to bake 20 to 25 minutes or until a knife inserted near center comes out clean.
- Cool on wire rack. Chill within two hours. Cover for longer storage.

Serves 8 to 10

Lemon Cheese Tarts

3 eggs
1 cup sugar
½ cup fresh lemon juice

2 teaspoons grated lemon zest
1 (8-ounce) package cream cheese, softened
12 tart shells

- Beat eggs in top of double boiler until thick and fluffy. Continue beating and gradually add sugar, lemon juice and zest. Place over hot water and cook, stirring constantly, until custard is thick and smooth; cool slightly.
- Gradually blend custard into cream cheese until smooth. Fill tart shells.

Makes 12 tarts

Coconut-Macadamia Nut Pie

½ (15-ounce) package refrigerated piecrusts
1 cup sugar
3 large eggs
1 cup light corn syrup
¼ cup whipping cream
1 tablespoon butter or margarine, melted

1 teaspoon vanilla extract
¾ cup coarsely chopped macadamia nuts
1 cup flaked coconut
Whipped cream for garnish
Chopped macadamia nuts for garnish
Toasted flaked coconut for garnish

- Preheat oven to 425°.

- Fit piecrust into 9-inch pie plate according to package directions; fold edges under, and crimp. Freeze piecrust 15 minutes.

- Bake piecrust 6 to 8 minutes or until golden; cool on a wire rack.

- Reduce oven temperature to 350°.

- Whisk together sugar, eggs, corn syrup, whipping cream, butter and vanilla; stir in nuts and coconut. Pour into prepared piecrust.

- Bake 55 to 60 minutes, cool on a wire rack. Garnish, if desired.

Makes 1 pie

Dried Cherry and Raisin Rice Pudding

1	cup water		2	large egg whites
¼	teaspoon salt		1	teaspoon vanilla extract
½	cup long-grain white rice		⅛	teaspoon ground cardamom
3	cups 1% fat milk		⅓	cup golden raisins
⅓	cup sugar		⅓	cup dried tart cherries
1	large egg			

- In a 2-quart heavy saucepan, bring water with salt to a boil; stir in rice. Cover pan and reduce heat to low, then cook until water is absorbed, about 15 minutes.

- Stir in milk and sugar; cook over very low heat, covered, until mixture resembles a thick soup, 50 minutes to 1 hour.

- Whisk together egg, egg whites, vanilla, cardamom and a pinch of salt. Whisk about 1 cup hot rice into egg mixture, then stir into remaining rice. Cook over low heat (do not boil), whisking constantly, until an instant-read thermometer registers 170°, 1 to 2 minutes.

- Remove from heat and stir in raisins and cherries.

- Transfer pudding to a 2-quart dish or 6 (8-ounce) ramekins; cover surface with wax paper and chill until cool but not cold, 1 to 2 hours.

Serves 6

Riverside Banana Pudding

2 (7.25-ounce) bags premium-quality buttery shortbread cookies

6-8 bananas, sliced

2 cups milk

1 (5-ounce) box instant French vanilla pudding

1 (8-ounce) package cream cheese, softened

1 (14-ounce) can sweetened condensed milk

1 (12-ounce) container frozen whipped topping, thawed, or equal amount sweetened whipped cream

- Line bottom of a 9 x 13 x 2-inch dish with 1 bag of cookies and layer bananas on top.

- In a bowl, combine milk and pudding mix; blend well using a handheld mixer. In a separate bowl, combine cream cheese and condensed milk together and mix until smooth. Fold whipped topping into cream cheese mixture.

- Add cream cheese mixture to pudding mixture and stir until well blended. Pour mixture over cookies and bananas and cover with remaining cookies.

- Refrigerate until ready to serve.

Serves 12

Note: This will become everyone's favorite recipe. Simple to make and unbelievably good.

Festive Fruit Pizza

Crust

¾ cup butter

½ cup confectioners' sugar

1½ cups all-purpose flour

Nonstick cooking spray

- Preheat oven to 300°.
- Cream butter; add sugar and flour and mix until dough forms into a ball. Pat into a 12-inch pizza pan sprayed with nonstick cooking spray. Bake 25 to 28 minutes or until crust just begins to brown. Cool.

Topping

10 ounces white chocolate chips

¼ cup heavy whipping cream

1 (8-ounce) package cream cheese, softened

Fresh fruit in season: bananas, strawberries, blueberries, peaches, kiwi

- Melt chocolate in double boiler or microwave; stir in cream until creamy. Add cream cheese and mix until well blended. Spread over cooled cookie crust.
- Refrigerate 30 minutes. Top with fruit.

Glaze

½ cup pineapple juice

¼ cup sugar

1 tablespoon cornstarch

½ teaspoon lemon juice

- In a saucepan, mix pineapple juice, sugar, cornstarch and lemon juice over medium heat until thickened. Brush over fruit topping with a pastry brush.
- Refrigerate at least 1 hour before serving.

Serves 12

Summer Lemon Mousse

½ cup water	Pinch salt
3-4 large lemons	½ cup heavy whipping cream
1 cup sugar	1-2 biscotti, crumbled for garnish
1 envelope unflavored gelatin	Fresh raspberries (optional)
4 large eggs, separated	Candied lemon peel for garnish
Ice cubes	

- Measure water into a small saucepan. Sprinkle in gelatin and let soften 5 minutes. Heat gently until gelatin dissolves.

- Grate zest of one lemon; place into a medium-sized metal bowl and add egg yolks with ¾ cup sugar. Whisk gelatin into egg yolk mixture and blend thoroughly.

- Place bowl over low heat and continue to cook until sugar dissolves and eggs start to thicken, about 5 minutes. Prepare a large bowl containing ice and water. Remove metal bowl from heat and place it in larger bowl of ice. Continue to beat until mixture cools.

- Squeeze 3 or more lemons to make ¾ cup juice. Whisk juice into yolk mixture. It should feel thick, like syrup. If not, let mixture continue to cool a few more minutes until thickened.

- In a separate bowl, beat egg whites with a pinch of salt until soft peaks form. Add remaining sugar and continue beating egg whites until they stand in firm peaks. In a third bowl, whip cream until it is thick but not too stiff.

- Stir about ¼ of egg whites into lemon-yolk mixture to lighten it, then fold in remaining egg whites and whipped cream. Divide mixture among 8 wine glasses, sherbet glasses or custard cups.

- Garnish with crumbled biscotti and/or fresh raspberries, if desired.

Serves 8

Melt-In-Your-Mouth Chocolate Mousse

1½	pounds semi-sweet chocolate morsels	¼	cup sugar
½	cup brewed espresso coffee	8	egg whites
½	cup Grand Marnier		Pinch salt
4	egg yolks	½	teaspoon vanilla extract
2	cups heavy or whipping cream, cold, divided		

- In a heavy saucepan, melt chocolate over very low heat, stirring constantly (or use double boiler). Add espresso then stir in Grand Marnier. Let mixture cool to room temperature.

- Add egg yolks, one at a time, beating thoroughly after each addition.

- Whip 1 cup of cream until thickened. Gradually add sugar, beating until cream is stiff.

- Beat egg whites with salt until soft peaks form. Gently fold egg whites into whipped cream.

- Stir in ⅓ of cream mixture thoroughly into chocolate mixture. Scrape remaining cream mixture over chocolate base, and gently fold them together. Pour mousse into individual dessert cups or a serving bowl and refrigerate 2 hours or until set. May be frozen and thawed before serving.

- At serving time, whip remaining 1 cup cream until thickened. Add vanilla and whip to soft peaks. Top each portion of mousse with a dollop of whipped cream and garnish as desired with chocolate leaves, candied flowers, chocolate shavings, etc.

Serves 8

Wine Jelly Dessert

2	tablespoons unflavored gelatin	⅓	cup sherry or Madeira wine
½	cup cold water	3	tablespoons lemon juice
1⅔	cups boiling water		Sweetened whipped cream
1	cup sugar		

- Soak gelatin in cold water 20 minutes, then add boiling water. Add sugar, wine and lemon juice. Pour into mold or individual parfait glasses.

- Chill until set. Serve with sweetened whipped cream.

Serves 4

Butter Pecan Ice Cream

1½-2 cups pecan pieces
3   tablespoons butter, melted
½   teaspoon salt
1   (14-ounce) can sweetened condensed milk
1   (12-ounce) can evaporated milk
1   tablespoon vanilla extract
2   teaspoons butter flavoring

¼-½ teaspoon maple flavoring
2   eggs
1   cup sugar
½   gallon whole milk
1   pint half & half
1   cup whipping cream

- Preheat oven to 325°.

- In the oven toast pecans in butter for 15 minutes. Watch closely and stir often. Sprinkle with ½ teaspoon salt and cool.

- Cream eggs and sugar. Mix in condensed milk, evaporated milk, vanilla extract, butter flavoring and maple flavoring.

- Pour into ice cream maker. Add half & half, cream and fill almost to top with whole milk, leaving enough space to sprinkle pecans on each side of dasher. Freeze.

Makes 1 gallon

Rum-Raisin Ice Cream

---

1 ¼	cups raisins
½	cup dark rum
3	cups milk
1	vanilla bean

1	cup sugar
9	egg yolks
	Ice cubes
2	cups whipping cream

- Combine raisins and rum in a small bowl; cover and let stand 8 hours.
- Cook milk and vanilla bean in a heavy saucepan over medium heat, stirring often, just until steaming. Remove from heat; cover and let stand 20 to 30 minutes. Remove vanilla bean; split in half lengthwise, scraping to remove seeds. Return seeds and pod to milk mixture.
- Whisk together sugar and egg yolks in a bowl until thick and pale. Gradually whisk in hot milk mixture; return to saucepan.
- Cook, whisking constantly, over medium-low heat until custard mixture thickens and will coat a spoon. (Do not overcook.)
- Pour custard mixture through a wire-mesh strainer into a medium bowl, discarding vanilla bean pod and seeds. Place bowl in a larger bowl filled with ice, and stir custard until cool.
- Pour raisin mixture through a wire-mesh strainer, discarding rum. Stir raisins and whipping cream into custard. Pour mixture into freezer container of a 5-quart hand-turned or electric freezer. Freeze according to manufacturer's instructions.
- Pack freezer with additional ice and rock salt, and let stand 1 hour before serving.

Makes 2 quarts

Scrumptious Mocha Ice Cream Dessert

24 chocolate cream sandwich cookies, crushed
⅓ cup butter, melted
½ gallon coffee ice cream
3 ounces unsweetened chocolate
2 tablespoons butter or margarine
1 cup sugar
Dash salt

2 (5½- to 6-ounce) cans evaporated milk
½ teaspoon vanilla extract
1½ cups heavy cream, whipped
1½ ounces Kahlúa liqueur
Confectioners' sugar to taste
½-¾ cup chopped nuts

- Combine cookie crumbs and butter. Press into the bottom of a buttered 13 x 9 x 2-inch pan. Refrigerate. When chilled, spoon on softened ice cream. Freeze.

- Melt chocolate and butter. Add sugar, salt and milk. Boil, stirring, until thickened. Remove from heat and add vanilla. Chill; spread on top of ice cream. Freeze.

- Whip cream. Add Kahlúa and confectioners' sugar to taste. Spread over chocolate layer and sprinkle with chopped nuts. Freeze.

Serves 25

Apple Dumplings

4 Granny Smith apples, peeled and cut into wedges
1 can flaky-type layer biscuits
1 stick butter

1½ cups water
1½ cups sugar

- Preheat oven to 350°.

- Divide each biscuit into 3 layers. Put 1 apple slice in each layer and fold over like a half moon. Place biscuits into a 13 x 9 x 2-inch pan.

- Boil butter, water and sugar until a syrup consistency forms. Pour syrup over biscuits (they will float). Sprinkle with cinnamon.

- Bake 30 minutes.

Serves 4-6

Peppermint Bark

6   red and white peppermint candy canes
1   (12-ounce) package semi-sweet chocolate chips

1   (10-ounce) package white baking chips

- Place candy canes between sheets of waxed paper and crush with a meat mallet.
- Line an 11 x 7 x 2-inch baking pan with foil (do not grease). In a 1-quart glass measuring cup, melt semi-sweet chocolate chips in microwave on HIGH power about 1½ minutes, until melted and smooth when stirred. Spread evenly in foil-lined pan. Refrigerate 5 minutes (don't let it firm up).
- Melt white baking chips in another 1-quart glass container in microwave on 50% POWER (not high) about 3½ minutes or longer, until melted and smooth when stirred. Watch carefully to avoid burning.
- Drizzle or drop blobs of melted white chocolate over semi-sweet chocolate in pan and then spread evenly, being very careful. Sprinkle top with crushed candy, pressing in gently with fingertips. Refrigerate until firm. When firm, remove from pan and cut into irregular shapes with sharp knife.

Variation: Make peanut butter cup, English toffee or other flavor candy bark by sprinkling white layer with 4 to 6 chopped candy bars of your choice.

Yields about 2 dozen

Slow Cooker Candy

1   (16-ounce) jar dry roasted unsalted peanuts
1   (16-ounce) jar dry roasted salted peanuts
1   (12-ounce) package semi-sweet chocolate chips

1   (4-ounce) German chocolate bar, broken into pieces
3   pounds white bark, broken into pieces

- Put all ingredients into a 4- or 5-quart crock pot in order listed. Cover and cook 3 hours on Low. Do not remove lid. Turn off and cool about 30 minutes. Mix well and drop by teaspoonfuls on wax paper. Cool.

Makes about 170 pieces

Cranberry Crunch

3	cups peeled, chopped apple	1	cup sugar
2	cups raw cranberries		

- Preheat oven to 325°.
- Mix apple and cranberries and place in buttered casserole. Pour sugar over mixture.

Topping

1½	cups uncooked oatmeal	1	cup butter, melted
½	cup brown sugar	1	cup chopped nuts
⅓	cup flour		

- Combine oatmeal, brown sugar, flour and butter. Sprinkle over fruit. Sprinkle nuts over top. Bake 1 hour or until golden.

Serves 4 to 6

The Best Bananas Ever

4	bananas	½	cup chopped almonds or macadamia nuts
½	cup brown sugar	2	tablespoons butter
¼	cup pineapple juice		Nutmeg to taste (optional)
3	tablespoons sherry		

- Preheat oven to 350°.
- Peel and place bananas in lightly buttered baking dish. Mix brown sugar, juice and sherry; pour over bananas.
- Sauté nuts in butter and sprinkle over bananas. Add a dash of nutmeg, if using.
- Bake about 15 to 20 minutes until tender and bananas are glazed. Spoon juice over bananas.

Serves 4

Note: Great served over ice cream.

Oatmeal Cranberry White Chocolate Chunk Cookies

1   cup butter or margarine
1   cup brown sugar
2   eggs
2   cups rolled oats
2   cups flour

½   teaspoon salt
1   teaspoon baking soda
1½ cups dried cranberries
1   cup white chocolate chunks

- Preheat oven to 375°.
- Using an electric mixer, beat butter and sugar together until light and fluffy. Add eggs and mix well.
- Combine oats, flour, salt and baking soda. Add to butter mixture a little at a time, mixing well after each addition. Stir in dried cranberries and white chocolate chunks.
- Drop by teaspoonfuls onto ungreased cookie sheets. Bake 10 to 12 minutes or until golden brown.

Makes 4 dozen cookies

Chocolate Mint Snaps

4   (1-ounce) squares unsweetened chocolate
1¼ cups butter
2   cups sugar
2   eggs
⅓   cup light corn syrup
2½ tablespoons water

2   teaspoons peppermint extract
1   teaspoon vanilla extract
4   cups all-purpose flour
2   teaspoons baking soda
½   teaspoon salt
    Sugar for rolling.

- Preheat oven to 350°.
- Using a double boiler, melt chocolate over hot water. Remove from heat.
- Cream butter, gradually adding 2 cups sugar, beating until light and fluffy. Add melted chocolate, eggs, corn syrup, water, peppermint extract and vanilla extract; mix well. Combine flour, soda and salt; add to creamed mixture, beating until just blended.
- Shape dough into 1-inch balls, and roll in remaining sugar. Place on ungreased cookie sheets; bake 10 minutes. Cool on cookie sheets 5 minutes. Remove to wire racks and cool completely.

Makes 10 dozen

Let's Get Together Cookies

1	cup butter or margarine, softened	1	teaspoon baking soda	
1	cup vegetable oil	1	teaspoon salt	
1	cup sugar	1	teaspoon cream of tartar	
1	cup firmly packed brown sugar	1	cup rolled oats, uncooked	
1	egg	1	cup crisp rice cereal	
2	teaspoons vanilla extract	1	(12-ounce) package semi-sweet chocolate morsels	
3½	cups all-purpose flour	¾	cup chopped pecans	

- Preheat oven to 375°.

- Cream butter and oil; gradually add sugars, beating at medium speed of an electric mixer. Add egg and vanilla, mixing well.

- Combine flour, soda, salt, and cream of tartar; gradually add to creamed mixture, mixing well. Stir in oats and remaining ingredients.

- Drop dough by teaspoonfuls onto greased cookie sheets. Bake 10 to 12 minutes. Cool on wire racks.

Makes 10 dozen cookies

Cinnamon, Spice and Everything Nice Cookies

1½ cups shortening

2 cups sugar

2 eggs

2 tablespoons vanilla extract

½ cup light molasses

4 cups all-purpose flour

4 teaspoons baking soda

2 teaspoons salt

2 teaspoons ground nutmeg

2 teaspoons ground ginger

1 (10-ounce) package cinnamon chips

1 cup sugar for decoration

- Preheat oven to 350°.

- In a large bowl, cream together shortening and 2 cups sugar until smooth. Beat in eggs, one at a time, then stir in vanilla and molasses.

- Combine flour, baking soda, salt, nutmeg and ginger; stir into sugar mixture until well blended. Mix in cinnamon chips. Dough will be stiff.

- Roll into walnut sized balls and roll each ball in remaining sugar. Place cookies 2 inches apart onto an ungreased cookie sheet and flatten slightly.

- Bake 8 to 10 minutes or until tops are crackled. Let cool on the baking sheet for a few minutes before removing to a wire rack to cool completely.

Makes 5 dozen cookies

White Chocolate Macadamia Nut Cookies

½ cup butter or margarine, softened
½ cup shortening
¾ cup firmly packed brown sugar
½ cup sugar
1 large egg
1½ teaspoons vanilla extract

2 cups all-purpose flour
1 teaspoon baking soda
½ teaspoon salt
1 (6-ounce) package white chocolate-flavored baking bars, cut into chunks
1 (7-ounce) jar macadamia nuts, coarsely chopped

- Preheat oven to 350°.
- Beat butter and shortening at medium speed with an electric mixer until soft and creamy; gradually add sugars, beating well. Add egg and vanilla; beat well.
- Combine flour, soda and salt; gradually add to butter mixture, beating well. Stir in white chocolate and nuts.
- Drop dough by rounded teaspoonfuls 2 inches apart onto lightly greased baking sheets.
- Bake 8 to 10 minutes or until lightly browned. Cool slightly on baking sheets; remove to wire racks, and let cool completely.

Makes 5 dozen cookies

Meltaway Cookies

4 sticks butter or margarine, softened
½ cup sugar
4 cups unsifted all-purpose flour

2 cups (12 ounces) chocolate chips (optional)
Confectioners' sugar for dusting (optional)

- Preheat oven to 350°. Cream butter and sugar in large bowl until light and creamy. Gradually add flour, then stir in chips.
- Roll well rounded teaspoonfuls of dough into balls and place on ungreased cookie sheets.
- Bake 12 minutes, cookies will still look pale. Dust with sugar, if desired.

Makes 4 to 6 dozen cookies

Debutante Praline Cookies

1⅔ cups all-purpose flour, sifted
1½ teaspoons baking powder
½   teaspoon salt
1¼ cups packed light brown sugar
1¼ cups packed dark brown sugar
1   stick unsalted butter, softened

1   large egg
1   teaspoon vanilla extract
½   cup (or more) heavy cream
1   cup sifted confectioners' sugar
1   cup pecan halves, toasted, coarsely chopped

- Preheat oven to 350°.
- Sift flour, baking powder and salt into a medium bowl. Mix light brown sugar and dark brown sugar in a separate bowl.
- Cream butter and 1½ cups brown sugar at medium speed of an electric mixer in a mixing bowl for 2 minutes or until light and fluffy. Beat in egg and vanilla. Add flour mixture and mix well at low speed.
- Drop by rounded teaspoonfuls 2 inches apart on ungreased cookie sheet. Bake 10 to 12 minutes or until golden brown. Cool in the pan for 5 minutes. Remove to wire rack to cool completely.
- Combine remaining brown sugar mixture with cream in a small saucepan. Bring to a boil over medium heat and cook 2 minutes, stirring constantly; remove from heat. Whisk in confectioners' sugar. Stir in pecans. Adjust consistency if necessary by adding a small amount of additional cream.
- Place cookies on wire rack over a lined baking pan. Spoon about ½ teaspoon of topping mixture over each cookie.

Makes 2½ dozen cookies

Lemon Blondies

Batter

1 cup all-purpose flour	¼ cup sugar
½ cup margarine	½ teaspoon vanilla extract

- Preheat oven to 350°.
- Blend flour, margarine, sugar and vanilla until well combined. Spread into greased 13 x 9 x 2-inch baking pan. Bake 12 minutes.

Topping

2 eggs	½ teaspoon salt
1½ cups brown sugar	1 teaspoon vanilla extract
1½ cups chopped pecans	1 lemon
2 tablespoons all-purpose flour	1½-2 cups confectioners' sugar

- Combine eggs, brown sugar, pecans, flour, salt and vanilla together. Spread onto batter. Bake at 350° for 25 minutes. Cool.
- Mix juice and zest of lemon with 1½ to 2 cups confectioners' sugar and pour on top of cooled brownies. Cut into 28 squares.

Makes 28 brownies

Crème de Menthe Brownies

Brownie

1	cup sugar
½	cup butter
4	eggs

1	cup all-purpose flour
½	teaspoon salt
16	ounces chocolate syrup

- Preheat oven to 350°.
- In a mixing bowl, blend sugar, butter, eggs, flour, salt and syrup together. Pour into greased 13 x 9 x 2-inch baking pan. Bake 25 to 30 minutes. Cool on a wire rack. (Top may appear wet.)

Mint Filling

2	cups confectioners' sugar
2	tablespoons crème de menthe

½	cup butter

- Mix together sugar, crème de menthe and butter until creamy and spread evenly over top of brownies.

Icing

6	ounces chocolate chips

6	tablespoons butter

- Melt chocolate and butter together and cool. Spread over mint layer. Refrigerate.
- Cut into squares after brownies have cooled but before they are too hard.

Variation: You may mix together 1 tablespoon water, ½ teaspoon mint extract and 3 drops green food color and substitute for crème de menthe.

Yields about 4 dozen

Pineapple Brownies with Cream Cheese Frosting

2 cups crushed pineapple, undrained
2 cups sugar
2 cups all-purpose flour
2 teaspoons baking soda

2 eggs
1 teaspoon ground cinnamon
1 cup pecans or walnuts, chopped

- Preheat oven to 325°.

- In a mixing bowl, combine pineapple, sugar, flour, soda, eggs, cinnamon and nuts; mix well. Pour into a greased and floured 13 x 9 x 2-inch pan and bake 35 minutes. Cool. Spread Cream Cheese Frosting over brownies and chill. Slice into squares. Store refrigerated.

Cream Cheese Frosting

1 (8-ounce) package cream cheese, softened
¾ stick butter

1 teaspoon vanilla extract
1 (1-pound) box confectioners' sugar

- Cream cheese and butter together. Add vanilla, then sugar and mix until creamy.

Yields about 20 squares

Lemon-Lime Blueberry Squares

Crust

½	cup all-purpose flour
¼	cup yellow cornmeal
6	tablespoons confectioners' sugar

½	teaspoon salt
1	stick cold unsalted butter, cut into pieces

- Preheat oven to 375°. Line a buttered 8 x 8 x 2-inch square glass baking dish with 2 (18 x 6-inch) sheets of foil, overlapping them in opposite directions so there is overhang on all 4 sides.

- Pulse together flour, cornmeal, confectioners' sugar, salt and butter in a food processor until mixture resembles coarse meal. Press onto bottom of baking dish and 1 inch up sides. Bake in middle of oven until golden brown, about 20 minutes.

Filling

3	large eggs
½	cup sugar
1½	tablespoons flour
½	teaspoon finely grated lemon zest
1	tablespoon fresh lemon juice

½	teaspoon finely grated lime zest
1	tablespoon fresh lime juice
2	tablespoons whole milk
2	cups blueberries
3	tablespoons apricot jam, heated and strained

- Whisk together eggs, sugar, flour and zests. Whisk in juices, milk and a pinch of salt. Toss blueberries with jam in another bowl.

- Whisk egg mixture and immediately pour into hot crust, then bake until just set, about 17 minutes. Gently spoon berries evenly over top and bake 2 minutes. Transfer baking dish to a rack and cool.

- Chill, covered, 8 hours or overnight. Use foil to lift dessert out of dish, then cut into squares.

Makes 9 squares

Cranberry Dream Bars

1   cup butter, softened
¾   cup sugar
¾   cup firmly packed brown sugar
2   eggs
1   teaspoon vanilla extract

2¼   cups all-purpose
1   teaspoon baking powder
1   (12-ounce) package white chocolate chips
1   (6-ounce) package sweetened dried cranberries
1   cup coarsely chopped macadamia nuts

- Preheat oven to 350°.
- Combine butter, sugar and brown sugar in a large mixing bowl. Beat with an electric mixer on medium speed until well blended. Add eggs and vanilla and beat well.
- Combine flour and baking powder; gradually add to mixture. Stir in chocolate chips, cranberries and macadamia nuts. Spread dough evenly in greased 15½ x 10½ x 1-inch jelly-roll pan.
- Bake 20 minutes or until light golden brown. Do not overbake.

Makes 4 dozen bars

English Toffee

1   pound ~~peanut~~ butter
2   tablespoons water
2   cups sugar

½   teaspoon salt
2   cups finely chopped walnuts, divided
1   (8-ounce) bar milk chocolate

- A candy thermometer must be used for this recipe.
- Combine butter and water in a 4-quart Dutch oven and cook over medium heat until butter melts. Add sugar and salt, mixing well. Bring to a boil, stirring constantly. Boil gently until mixture reaches 300°. Remove from heat immediately and add 1 cup of nuts.
- Pour mixture into a buttered 15½ x 10½ x 1-inch jelly-roll pan, spreading to edges of pan. When mixture has reached room temperature, melt chocolate and spread over top. Sprinkle with remaining nuts. Let stand until chocolate is firm. Break into pieces.

Makes about 3 pounds

Chewy Pecan Bars

Crust

1¾ cups all-purpose flour
⅔ cup confectioners' sugar
¼ cup cornstarch

½ teaspoon salt
1½ sticks cold unsalted butter, cut into ½-inch pieces

- Preheat oven to 350°.
- Line 13 x 9 x 2-inch pan with foil, leaving 1-inch overhang on all sides. Butter foil.
- Blend flour, sugar, cornstarch and salt in processor. Add butter and process until mixture begins to clump together.
- Press dough evenly onto bottom of foil-lined pan. Bake crust until set and light golden, about 25 minutes. Remove from oven. Let stand while preparing topping.
- Reduce oven temperature to 325°.

Topping

1¼ cups light brown sugar, packed
½ cup light corn syrup
¼ cup unsalted butter

4 cups coarsely chopped pecans
½ cup whipping cream
2 teaspoons vanilla extract

- Stir brown sugar, corn syrup and butter in a heavy medium saucepan over medium-high heat until sugar dissolves and mixture boils; boil 1 minute. Add pecans and cream; boil until mixture thickens slightly, about 3 minutes. Stir in vanilla. Pour hot topping over warm crust.
- Bake nut-topped crust until caramel is darker and bubbles thickly, about 20 minutes. Transfer pan to rack. Cool completely in pan. Topping will harden.
- Lift foil out of pan onto cutting board. Using heavy sharp knife, cut crust with nut topping into rectangles. (Can be made 1 week ahead; store between sheets of waxed paper in airtight container at room temperature.)

Yields 24

Note: You may use a mixer for crust. Butter should be room temperature or softened. Cream butter and sugar until blended, then add remaining ingredients. Mix until well blended.

Chocolate Sherry Cream Bars

Bars

4	ounces unsweetened baking chocolate
1	cup margarine
4	eggs
2	cups sugar

1	cup all-purpose flour
½	teaspoon salt
1	teaspoon vanilla

- Preheat oven to 350°.

- Using double boiler, melt chocolate and margarine over hot water, cool slightly. Beat eggs until light and fluffy. Cream in sugar. Add flour, salt and vanilla and beat 1 minute. Pour into greased and floured 13 x 9 x 2-inch baking pan. Bake 25 minutes. Cool.

Filling

½	cup butter
4	cups confectioners' sugar
¼	cup half & half

¼	cup sherry
1	cup chopped nuts

- Beat butter and sugar together and gradually add half & half and sherry. Should be light and fluffy. Mix in nuts. Spread over bars and chill.

Topping

1	(6-ounce) package semi-sweet morsels
4	tablespoons water

4	tablespoons butter

- Using double boiler, melt chocolate with butter and water over hot water. Mix well. Drizzle over filling. Chill until firm. Cut into 1-inch bars. Store in refrigerator.

Makes 5 dozen bars

Baklava

1-2 pounds walnuts and/or almonds
¾ cup sugar
2 teaspoons ground cinnamon
1 teaspoon allspice (optional)

1 pound sweet unsalted butter, do not substitute
1 pound phyllo dough
Whole cloves
Honey Syrup (recipe follows)

- Preheat oven to 350° or 300°.

- Chop nuts and mix with sugar and spice. Cut phyllo dough to fit a 13 x 9 x 2-inch baking pan. Brush pan with melted butter, place 8 to 10 phyllo sheets in bottom of pan, brushing each with melted butter.

- Cover with a thin layer of nut mixture. Cover with one phyllo sheet, apply melted butter, and sprinkle with nut mixture. Continue to place alternately one phyllo sheet, treated with melted butter, and one layer of nut mixture until you have only 6 phyllo sheets left.

- Place remaining 6 phyllo sheets on top of one another to form the top of the baklava and brush each sheet with melted butter. With a sharp knife dipped in hot butter, cut baklava into strips 1½-inches wide and cut these strips diagonally to form small diamond-shaped pieces. A clove may be placed in the center of each piece.

- Heat remaining butter and pour into the knife slits. Bake at 350° for 40 minutes or 1 hour at 300°. When baklava is evenly browned, remove from oven and pour cooled syrup evenly over it, so that it penetrates the layers and covers the baklava. Allow to cool several hours before serving.

Honey Syrup
1 cup sugar
1 cup water

1½ cups honey
2 teaspoons vanilla

- Cook sugar and water over low heat until a syrup consistency, about 10 minutes. Add honey and vanilla and cook for 5 minutes longer. Cool.

Yields 4 dozen

Note: Thaw phyllo ahead according to package directions. While working with phyllo sheets, keep dough covered with a damp dish towel or plastic wrap as it can dry out very fast. Keep butter warm as it spreads easier and less is used. Use a pastry brush for quickly wetting phyllo with butter. The better quality honey used, the better the baklava will be. Use all the honey syrup. The pastry will appear to be swimming in syrup, but it is slowly absorbed. Keeps well and flavor seems to improve each day, so can be made ahead.

Raspberry Ripple

2 cups flour
1 cup butter
½ cup sugar
⅛ teaspoon salt
1 egg yolk, beaten

½ cup raspberry jam
¼ cup sliced almonds
½ teaspoon vanilla extract
Confectioners' sugar

- Preheat oven to 350°.

- Combine flour, butter, sugar and salt with a pastry blender until consistency of coarse meal. Add egg yolk and work with hands until mixture forms a ball. Divide mixture into thirds.

- On an ungreased cookie sheet, shape each third into a 12 x 1-inch strip; place strips 4 inches apart. With the back of a spoon, make a depression about ½-inch deep along the length of each strip.

- Combine raspberry jam, almonds and vanilla. Spread ⅓ of jam mixture into each strip. Refrigerate 30 minutes. Bake for 15 to 20 minutes, or until golden.

- Cool slightly on cookie sheet, then cut diagonally into 2-inch wide pieces. Finish cooling on a wire rack. Sprinkle lightly with confectioners' sugar.

Makes 3 dozen

Viennese Coffee Balls

2 cups crushed shortbread cookies
1¼ cups sifted confectioners' sugar, divided
1 cup finely chopped nuts
2 tablespoons unsweetened cocoa powder

1½ teaspoons instant coffee crystals or instant espresso powder
¾ teaspoon ground cinnamon
4-5 tablespoons brewed espresso or strong coffee, or water
Sifted confectioners' sugar (optional)

- Combine crushed cookies, 1¼ cups confectioners' sugar, nuts, cocoa, coffee crystals and cinnamon. Add brewed espresso, coffee or water, using just enough to moisten.
- Form mixture into 1¼-inch balls. Roll balls generously in confectioners' sugar. Place balls on a sheet of waxed paper; let stand until dry, about 1 hour.
- Before serving, roll balls again in confectioners' sugar, if desired.

Makes 30 balls

Note: To store balls, place in layers separated by waxed paper in an airtight container; cover. Store at room temperature for up to 3 days or freeze for up to 3 months.

Pecan Triangles

1   cup butter, softened
1   cup sugar
1   egg, separated

2   cups sifted all-purpose flour
1   teaspoon ground cinnamon
1   cup finely chopped pecans

- Preheat oven to 275°.
- Cream together butter and sugar. Add egg yolk; beat well.
- Sift together flour and cinnamon. Gradually add to creamed mixture, stirring well.
- Spread dough evenly into a 15½ x 10½ x 1-inch jelly-roll pan. Smooth surface with fingertips.
- Beat egg white slightly; brush over top.
- Sprinkle nuts over dough and press in.
- Bake in very slow oven 1 hour.
- While uncut cookie is still hot, cut into 4 lengthwise strips and then cut 6 crosswise strips. Cut each piece in half diagonally to make triangles.

Makes 4 dozen

Contributors

We are grateful to the following Active and Sustaining members of the Junior Charity League of Shelby, Inc. who generously contributed their resources, time, talent, and energy.

Sheila Allen
Marywinn Amaya
Altman Anderson
Candy Arey
Carole Arey
Lorraine Arey
Darlene Bailey
Montrose Ballard
Gracie Bankhead
Sally Barker
Cornelia Barnett
Ann Beam
Harriette Beam
Mary Beam
Tonya Beam
Amy Berry
Cindy Binion
Neal Binion
Janice Blake
Chrystal Blalock
Nancy Blanton
Laura Bonino
Flossie Bonner
Josie Bowles
Betty Bowling
Susan Bowling
Joyce Boyette

Sara Branton
Carol Bridges
Elizabeth Bridges
Kathryn Bridges
Linda Bridges
Marsha Brown
Jacquie Brunnick
Terre Bullock
Franki Burch
Kathie Burgin
Cathy Burns
Kim Burton
Robin Burton
Terri Byers
Amber Camp
Mariel Camp
Frances Campbell
Lynn Carter
Kay Chitty
Beth Clark
Penny Corn
Adelaide Craver
Mary Crawley
Zanne Crosland
Pat Crum
Greer Dalton
Mary Jane Darr

Helen Davis
LouAnne Davis
Jan Dedmon
Susan DuBose
Carolyn Durrett
Doris Edwards
Joan Edwards
Ann Elliott
Betsy Ellis
Patti Ellis
Polly Ellis
Pat Ellison
Catherine Eusebio
Fran Evans
Debbie Ferrell
Bitsy Fesperman
Ellen Fletcher
Joan Flowers
Danna Floyd
Esther Ann Ford
Jesse Forney
Kathy Gardner
Alison Gilbert
Carolyn Goforth
Linda Goforth
Peggy Goforth
Lorah Gold

A River's Course

Anne Goss
Wendi Gragg
Debbie Griffin
Karen Hall
Edith Hamilton
Margaret Hamrick
Mary Etta Hamrick
Sara Ellen Hamrick
Rita Hamrick
Betty Harris
Ann Harry
Susan Haskell
Angela Heath
Melissa Hendee
Carol Henry
Marilyn Henshaw
Becky Hill
Jerri Horn
Carol Ann Hudson
Sharon Hudson
Ruby Hunt
Suzanne Hunter
Helen Jeffords
Martha Johnson
Rebecca Johnson
Mary Jones
Millie Keeter-Holbrook
Mary Kelly
Jan Kendrick
Anne Kennedy
Maxine Kennedy
Nancy Kennedy

Doris Kiger
Vickie Knapp
Jean Konitzer
Connie Lackey
Beth Lari
Kim Lee
Jean LeGrand
Margaret Litton
Virginia Love
Brenda Lowery
Kaye Lowery
Carolyn Lutz
Claudia Lutz
Sue Lutz
Joan Mabry
Leigh Mabry
Susan Mabry
Susie Mabry
Mimi Martin
Sue Mauney
Debi McDaniel
Julianne McDowell
Barbara McLarty
Debbie McMurry
Louise McMurry
Patti McMurry
Loann Meekins
Lydia Miller
Wendy Mode
Emily Monroe
Kathryn Monroe
Keely Monroe

Alison Moore
Barbara Moore
Rhonda Moore
Barbara Morgan
Eleanor Morgan
Jodi Morgan
Page Morgan
Mary Lou Moss
Gloria Newman
Martha Noblitt
Sharon Owens
Laura Kay Padgett
Virginia Padgett
Peggy Paksoy
Ellen Palmer
Julia Palmer
Adelyn Parker
Mary Parsons
Anne Pasco
Frankie Patterson
Linda Phillips
Brownie Plaster
Cassie Plaster
Lisa Poage
Becky Powell
Debbie Powell
Dawn Price
Julia Price
Kay Price
Mitzi Price
Laura Randle
Cathy Rempson

Contributors

Evelyn Ribadeneyra
Shelley Roberts
Janet Roebuck
Rita Rogers
Carol Rose
Claudia Rose
Jennifer Rose
Patsy Rose
Inez Rowan
Shana Runge
Connie Rupprecht
Zuzana Rybnicek
Nancy Surratt
Joanne Schenck
Becca Schweppe
Ruth Schweppe
Stuart Schweppe
Ginger Secrest
Grace Sheppard
Page Sherer
Anne Short
Kay Sipe
Frances Sizemore
Becky Smith
Laura Smith

Robin Smith
Evelyn Spangler
Lynn Spangler
Jeanne Spragins
Lisa Stachowicz
Jacky Stone
Martha Strain
Pat Taranto
Ann Taylor
Sally Taylor
Helen Tedder
Kim Tedder
Becky Teddy
Cindy Teddy
Linda Thompson
Peg Thornburg
Sara Tidwell
Che Tiernan
Nancy Tillman
Helen Toole
Mary Esther Toole
Lisa Trice
Beth Triplett
Janis Tucker
Suzanne Turner

Jill Venable
Lucy Ward
Teresa Warrick
Jackie Weathers
Judy Westmoreland
Linda White
Jody Wilkins
Mimi Wilkins
Gene Williams
Stephanie Williams
Sally Wills
Lynn Wise
Angie Wood
Carol Wood
Millie Wood
Kathy Woody
Anne Wray
Annette Wray
Mary Wray
Sarah Wray
June Yarboro
Emily Yelton
Martha Yelton
Connie Young
Jane Young

Just as rivers affect the land they flow over, the Junior Charity League of Shelby, Inc. has sought to influence the community it serves. The organization has been a part of the Cleveland County, North Carolina landscape since its inception in 1934. Those early years found ladies diligently serving the community in a variety of ways. Members assisted the Red Cross, sponsored a tubercular clinic, and provided help to polio victims. During the World War II era League members contributed to the war effort by serving as hostesses to soldiers away from home, worked as blood bank collectors, and acted as correspondents.

This spirit of service continues today. Each year the need grows to continue and expand the two main on-going service projects: The Clothing Room and "Kids on the Block." "Kids on the Block" is a puppet show dealing with many important issues facing children today. Performed for every third grade class in the county, this traveling troupe tackles the issues of child abuse, drug awareness, mental and physical handicaps, divorce and learning disabilities. Another important service project is The Clothing Room. Hundreds of disadvantaged children benefit from this service every year. Children are not only given new clothes and coats, but a renewed sense of self-worth. This avenue of service grows every year, seeing almost 800 children clothed in the 2003-2004 League year. Through these and other outreach services, all money raised is put back into the community.

None of the beneficial services that the League provides would be possible without the community's support in our fund raising efforts. This cookbook is our latest endeavor in that field. Our community, over the years, has enjoyed the culinary talents of our League members through Designer House tea rooms, holiday bake sales, Boxed Lunch sales, and Debutante Ball luncheons and receptions. It is our hope that combining these and other favorite recipes in a beautiful, well-designed book will benefit both the consumer and the community. Thank you for you continued support.

A River's Course

A GOURMET COLLECTION
of
The Junior Charity League of Shelby, Inc.

Name: _____

Address: _____

_____

City/State: _____

Zip: _____ Phone: _____

Quantity:	_____
Price per book:	$19.95
Shipping	_____
($4.00 per book)	
TOTAL	$_____

Send check or money order to:

The Junior Charity League of Shelby, Inc.

P.O. Box 1325

Shelby, North Carolina 28150

Internet Orders & Inquiries please contact: www.jclshelby.com

- -

A River's Course

A GOURMET COLLECTION
of
The Junior Charity League of Shelby, Inc.

Name: _____

Address: _____

_____

City/State: _____

Zip: _____ Phone: _____

Quantity:	_____
Price per book:	$19.95
Shipping	_____
($4.00 per book)	
TOTAL	$_____

Send check or money order to:

The Junior Charity League of Shelby, Inc.

P.O. Box 1325

Shelby, North Carolina 28150

Internet Orders & Inquiries please contact: www.jclshelby.com